TREASURES OF THE WORLD

COLLECTION PLANNED AND DIRECTED BY

ALBERT SKIRA

TREASURES
OF
TURKEY

THE EARLIEST CIVILIZATIONS OF ANATOLIA
BYZANTIUM
THE ISLAMIC PERIOD

EKREM AKURGAL
CYRIL MANGO
RICHARD ETTINGHAUSEN

SKIRA

Text of Ekrem Akurgal translated from
the original German by Robert Allen

★

© 1966 by Editions d'Art Albert Skira, Geneva
Library of Congress Catalog Card Number: 66-22488

★

PRINTED IN SWITZERLAND

CONTENTS

BULGARIA

GREECE

• Edirne

B L A C

Sino

Istanbul

Sea of Marmara

Kyzikos • Iznik

Kızılırmak

Ç

• Troy

Lake Manyas • Bursa

Sakarya

Ankara

Boğazköy Ala

Eskişehir

Yazılıkaya

Kütahya

Gordion

Pergamum

Midas Şehri

Kırşehir

Çandarlı

Aizani

Afyon Kara Hisar

Salt Lake

K

Sardis

Izmir (Smyrna)

Claros

Ephesus Tralles

Eğridir Lake

Beyeşhir Lake

Aksaray

Ürgü

Niğ

Priene

Hierapolis

Konya

Sultanhanı

Magnesia

Miletus

Didyma

Aphrodisias

Hacılar

Çatal höyük

Iasos

Kubadabad

Beyşehir

Karaman

Termessos Perga Aspendos

Antalya Side

Mersin

Cnidus

Xanthos

Finike

Alahan

Silifke

M E D I T E R R A N E A N S E A

S E A

un

Trebizond

asya

U S S R

Ani

Sivas

Erzincan

Erzurum

Ararat

Divriği

Malazgirt

Lake Van

IRAN

Malatya

Van

Bitlis

Aght'amar

Nimrud Dağ

Diyarbakır

Maraş

Euphrotes

Tigris

Sakçegözü

Mardin

Nusaybin

Urfa

IRAQ

Zincirli

Harran

be

takya

S Y R I A

THE
EARLIEST CIVILIZATIONS
OF ANATOLIA

HATTIC CULT STANDARD IN THE FORM OF A BRONZE STAG WITH SILVER HEAD AND ANTLERS AND SILVER INLAYS ON THE BODY.
FROM ALACA HÖYÜK, ABOUT 2300-2100 B.C. OVERALL HEIGHT 20½″. ARCHAEOLOGICAL MUSEUM, ANKARA.

PREHISTORIC ANATOLIA

The prehistory of Anatolia remained clothed in the deepest mystery until recent excavations brought to light cultural relics of outstanding importance. We know now that one of the major centers of prehistoric times was situated to the south of the Anatolian plateau. The Turkish archaeologists Kiliç Kökten and Enver Bostancı have discovered settlements in caves at Karain Belbaşı and Beldibi near Antalya, some of which date back to the Upper Palaeolithic era. The next oldest settlements in Anatolia are the Mersin mound excavated by John Garstang and the occupation levels at Hacılar and Çatal Höyük laid bare by James Mellaart. The fascinating, unique mural paintings and sculptures found at the last-named sites mark them as the culminating point of Neolithic culture in Anatolia. The highest level at Beldibi yielded primitive pottery very closely related to the oldest clay vessels found at Çatal Höyük. Carbon 14 dating has proved that the earliest settlement at Çatal Höyük was established about 6500 B.C., therefore those in the caves near Antalya must date back to the eighth millennium at least.

The people who lived there—except for the last phase at Beldibi I have just mentioned —had as yet no knowledge of pottery. Like those of the lowest levels at Hacılar established about 7000 B.C. and the other pre-ceramic Stone Age cultures, they must have used bowls of stone and wood. They had not attained the stage of agriculture and lived chiefly by hunting. But the wall paintings at Beldibi and Karain prove that Pamphylia enjoyed a relatively advanced way of life during the Upper Palaeolithic era. The first traces of agriculture were found in level V at Hacılar, which carbon 14 dating sets at about 7040 B.C. Stores of foodstuffs, such as wheat, barley and lentils, were found in the houses there and the debris of meals contained bones of goats, sheep and horned cattle. The only domestic animal of which there is any trace is the dog. Çatal Höyük, where twelve superimposed occupation levels dating approximately from 6500 to 5500 B.C. have been distinguished, turned out to be a unique center of prehistoric culture in which man produced his first really important works of art.

The finest of these are the paintings and painted reliefs that formerly adorned the walls of houses and shrines and are now kept in the Ankara Museum. The shrines were surrounded by a cluster of four or five houses, each of which as a rule comprised a number of large rooms. Neither the houses nor the shrines had doors and could only be entered through the roof with the help of wooden ladders. Both had the same ground-plan and were built of sun-dried bricks, with small windows let into the walls high up just below the gutter. Each dwelling room had at least two raised pavements. The main pavement was reinforced round the edges with timber and its polished surface was painted red. At one end was a bench that served as a divan on which the inmates could sit, work and sleep. The bones of the dead were interred under this bench after the flesh had been removed. Valuable offerings were placed in the graves: for instance, that of a woman yielded a magnificent obsidian mirror. In a shrine in level VII, which carbon 14 dating set at about 6200 B.C., there was a wall painting apparently representing the eruption of a volcano, probably Hasan Dağ that rises close by. This picture is the most ancient landscape painting we know of. The polychrome mural paintings have a great variety of subjects. The favorites were hunting scenes, pictures of dancers and acrobats, and in particular representations of religious and funeral rites.

These domestic shrines were probably used for the religious ceremonies connected with a fertility cult. One is struck by the enormous number of bulls' heads and horns set in rows on the walls or at the ends of the bench or raised pavement. They presumably represented the male deity. For the Anatolian farmers viewed the bull not only

PAINTED RELIEF WITH TWO LEOPARDS FROM A SHRINE IN LEVEL VI, ÇATAL HÖYÜK.
ABOUT 6000 B.C. ARCHAEOLOGICAL MUSEUM, ANKARA.

CLAY FIGURE OF A GODDESS ENTHRONED ON TWO FELINES AND GIVING BIRTH TO A CHILD. LEVEL II, ÇATAL HÖYÜK, ABOUT 5750 B.C.
(HEADS OF GODDESS AND ONE FELINE RESTORED) HEIGHT WITHOUT THE HEAD 6½″. ARCHAEOLOGICAL MUSEUM, ANKARA.

as a symbol of strength and fertility but even more as the begetter of the oxen without which they could not till their land. That is why from the start of husbandry the male deity was usually portrayed as a bull and only rarely in human form. This custom continued, as we shall see, into the Hittite period.

The only human figure in the painted stucco reliefs from Çatal Höyük is the Great Mother. But she too is often represented by her sacred beasts, the panther and the leopard. Two leopards on a richly colored stucco relief that adorned the wall of a shrine in level VI, about 6000 B.C., may be viewed as symbols of the mighty goddess. That they were really her own personal attributes is proved by a statuette that shows her enthroned on two catlike beasts. In that work she is portrayed bringing a child into the world—a motif typical of the Great Mother and frequently treated in the small sculptures from Hacılar. Statuettes found at Çatal Höyük also represent the goddess attending the birth of a bull's or ram's head. Another mural relief from level VII at Çatal Höyük apparently depicts a pregnant goddess because her navel is particularly stressed by two concentric circles. Childbirth and the bull, or his head, are typical symbols of fertility.

It is symptomatic that fertility symbols predominate in shrines where the dead are buried. They serve to comfort the bereaved as tokens of rebirth or perhaps even of life in the other world. This concept reappears five thousand years later in nearby Lycia, on the Harpy Monument where departed and votaries hold other fertility symbols—an egg, a cock or a pomegranate—in their hands to ease their hearts of despair for the dead and strengthen their belief that after death they are born again. Thus the earliest known representations of ancestor worship in painting and sculpture were found in the shrines at Çatal Höyük. The plump clay statuettes from Çatal Höyük and Hacılar are very eloquent. A favorite subject is the figure of a naked woman in various postures: lying on her side, kneeling, sleeping or giving birth to a child. Isolated male figures are seldom found. One is the oldest version of the "God on the Bull," a theme that occurs in Anatolia well into the Roman period. The male figure appears more frequently in hierogamic scenes tightly enlaced with a female figure.

We have already seen that the first clay vessels made in Anatolia date back to the earliest period at Çatal Höyük, about 6500 B.C. It is from there that the pottery found in the uppermost level at Beldibi must have come. The plain monochrome ware of early Neolithic type gradually blossomed in late Neolithic and early Chalcolithic times into a splendid ceramic art.

Painted clay vessels of unparalleled beauty were brought to light in the two highest occupation levels at Hacılar, which carbon 14 dating ascribes to 5400-5250 B.C. An almost identical ceramic art had long been known from Sesklo in Thessaly (Greece), where clay figurines like the small sculptures from Çatal Höyük and Hacılar were popular. But Asia Minor was the real center of this grand artistic trend; in fact, however much we may prize them, the works found at Sesklo are rather peripheral phenomena compared with the Anatolian finds. James Mellaart, who discovered and excavated the Neolithic settlements in Anatolia, made accessible to scholars a prehistoric culture that may well be termed the first truly great achievement of mankind.

In Anatolia the Chalcolithic period, in which stone and metal implements and artefacts occur side by side, begins in level V at Hacılar, dated by the carbon 14 test at about 5500 B.C. That was Hacılar's heyday, whose artistic production has been given its due above. The important finds from Can Hasan excavated by David French belong to the same period.

The late Chalcolithic was marked by a period of stagnation that lasted through the fifth and fourth millennia. The best works from that age come from the diggings at Beycesultan carried out by Seton Lloyd. Nearly two thousand years of pause had serious consequences for, after playing the lead in the seventh and sixth millennia, Anatolia fell politically and culturally far behind Mesopotamia right up to the second millennium. When writing was discovered in Egypt and the Near East about 3000 B.C. and the eastern nations attained their cultural peak, the whole of Anatolia was still bogged down in a prehistoric village culture.

The Turkish archaeologist Hamit Koşay discovered several important centers of this halting late Chalcolithic culture in central and western Anatolia and brought to light some beautifully shaped, highly polished monochrome pottery which is of remarkable quality despite the primitive living conditions in the small settlements where it was produced. The most important pieces were discovered at Alishar, where diggings were carried out by an American expedition under the leadership of H. H. von der Osten.

Even during the first phase of the Bronze Age, which lasted in Anatolia from about 3000 to 2500 B.C., the cities in the center and east of the peninsula did not experience any noteworthy development as compared with the late Chalcolithic. Therefore in Anatolia that phase should really be counted as part of the late Chalcolithic.

What is instead worthy of note is the establishment of the first Trojan settlement, which reveals close links with the early Bronze Age world on the Aegean coast and the Cyclades and differs greatly from the ancient culture of the Anatolian centers. As Carl Blegen observed, House 102 excavated at Troy displays all the characteristic features of a *megaron* and is clearly related to the West. It should be noted that the megaron-like edifice in level XI at Jericho in Palestine has no connection with the *megara* at Troy and Dimini. The extensive remains of the first enclosure wall of Troy show that it must have been an extremely effective fortification in its day.

It is only in the middle of the third millennium that we see a change take place in Anatolia. That was when the Bronze Age really began there. At that time the plateau was inhabited by a people whose name we know from later Hittite sources. They were the Hatti, who gave their name to Asia Minor from the beginning of the Akkadian dynasty (2350-2150 B.C.) to the days of the Assyrian kings of the late eighth century B.C. Even the Hittites named their empire the Land of Hatti and, although they were really called Nesians, are known to historians by a term derived from the Hatti. Only a few remnants of the language, Hatti-li, have been preserved. It differs from all the other known languages of Asia Minor and the Near East.

The Hattic influence can also be discerned in the ensuing Hittite period in religion and mythology, State ritual and court etiquette. Hattusas, capital of the Hittites, was originally, as its name indicates, a Hattic settlement. The strong Hattic traits of the Hittite culture demonstrate clearly that those prehistoric people could boast a high intellectual standard. They are the first civilized nation of that age outside Mesopotamia whose name we know and with whose language and religion we have a certain acquaintance. The finest works of art of that period come from the region in which the Hattic civilization was centered. Thirty years ago the Turkish archaeologists Remzi Oğuz Arik and Hamit Koşay discovered in the royal tombs at Alaca Höyük, not far from Hattusas, objects in gold, silver and bronze of such extraordinary beauty and quality that they put Schliemann's "Treasure of Priam" in the shade and brought Bronze Age Anatolia into the forefront of historical research.

They included some chalices technically very accomplished, pieces of jewelry of various kinds, and objects cast in bronze, inlaid with gold and silver. The ceremonial "standard"—a bronze stag with silver head and antlers and body patterned in silver inlay—must have deeply impressed the believers of the Land of Hatti in the course of religious rites. The stag was the theriomorphic embodiment of Wurusemu, the chief goddess of the Land of Hatti. At that time, just as four thousand years before at Çatal Höyük, her consort, the weather god, was worshipped exclusively in the shape of a bull. At Alaca Höyük the excavators found several statuettes of bulls wrought with the same technique and in the same shape as the Stag Standard reproduced here. The theriomorphic images of the deities were presumably mounted on pieces of furniture resembling canopies or thrones. Typical of these animal figures are the sloping back, elongated body and long, narrow muzzle. Though the shape of the body is stylized and abstracted, its major traits are naturalistically rendered. A fondness for ornamental decoration has given these little figures a naive charm that is most engaging.

The same royal tombs at Alaca Höyük yielded some curious standards shaped like the solar disk. They were mounted on poles with straps or cords and borne by the priests during religious ceremonies. The British Museum has some standards of the same type that came from modern churches in Ethiopia.

HATTIC CULT STANDARD SYMBOLIZING THE COSMOS. BRONZE. ON THE RIM, TWELVE BLOSSOMS; AT THE TOP, THREE BIRDS IN FLIGHT; AT THE BASE, A PAIR OF BULL'S HORNS. FROM ALACA HÖYÜK, ABOUT 2300-2100 B.C. HEIGHT 13½″. ARCHAEOLOGICAL MUSEUM, ANKARA.

These standards, at once mysterious and impressive, are cosmic symbols. It is hard to believe that the gloriole that adorns some of these disks and their curved shape, which recalls the vault of heaven, are mere ornamentation. The birds in flight on the rim of the disk on one standard may also well be a token of celestial significance. By analogy the blossoms that adorn the rim may symbolize plant life, which springs from the earth and grows heavenwards. The spreading bull's horns that serve as a base are fitted in such a way that they enclose the lower part of the standard and bear it aloft just as the bull-men bear aloft the symbol of heaven on the reliefs at Yazılıkaya carved in the thirteenth century B.C. These bulls' horns recall the Turkish fairytale that tells how the earth rests on the horns of an ox and quakes whenever the beast shakes its head. The precious standards of the Hattic priest kings may well be the first figurations of that idea.

A masterpiece of Hattic art is the unique silver statuette from Hasanoğlan near Ankara. Since it was discovered by chance and presumably came from a tomb, we have no stratigraphic reference point for this work. But its style is unmistakably Hattic. The rippling waves of the hair round the crown of the head occur in almost identical form on the gold vessels found in the royal tombs at Alaca Höyük. The covering of the neck with small beaten gold plates is also typical of Hattic goldsmiths' work; one of the bronze statuettes of bulls from Alaca Höyük has the neck plated with silver in the same way. The minute spherical breasts and buttonlike navel, both inlaid with gold, also recall the idols and figurines from the tombs there. The dotted pubic triangle, the gold bands crossed on chest and back, and in particular the exaggeratedly elongated neck are further stylistic factors that link the work from Hasanoğlan with the idol sculptor's art at an advanced stage of the early Bronze Age in Anatolia.

The statuette from Hasanoğlan with its big hooked nose gives us a good idea of the ethnic type of that time. A Hatti princess might have looked like that. We find the same facial type later in Hittite art. The majority of the inhabitants of central and eastern Anatolia very probably preserved a strongly Hattic cast of features well into the thirteenth century B.C.

The treatment of the body as a whole is not an unqualified success. There is a lack of proportion in the short legs, the low-slung hips, the overlong trunk and the knoblike breasts placed on a level with the shoulders. But these norms might be in keeping with the stylistic criteria of the idol sculptor's art that set the fashion in the last quarter of the third millennium. In other respects the goldsmith endeavored to overstep the bounds of tradition. But he only put his skill to the test in places that do not catch the eye. For instance, the modelling of the buttocks denotes a keen observation of nature and a great artistic talent. He may well have been familiar with the naturalistic sculpture of contemporary Mesopotamian artists. On the whole, his work is a blend of old and new. The hands resting on the stomach, with their long fingers and many

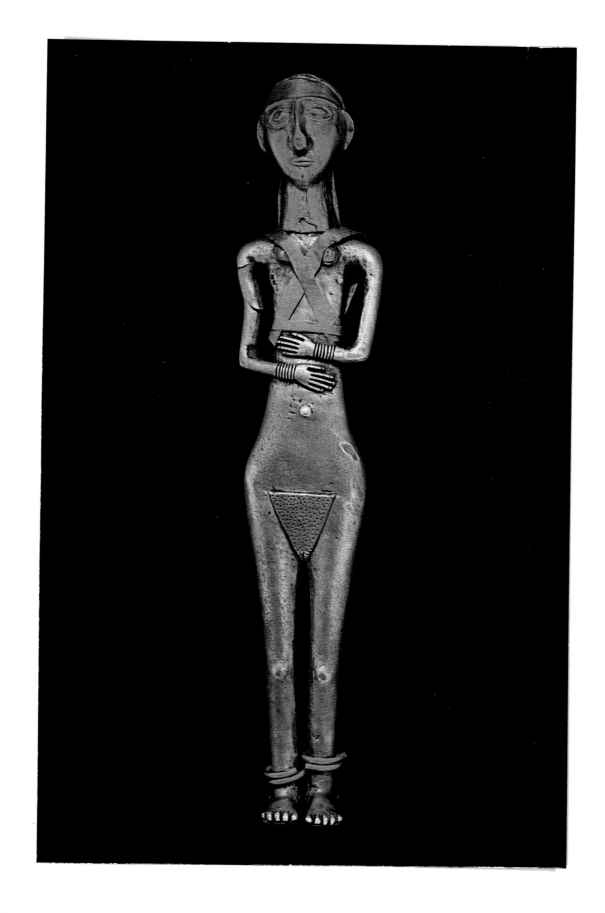

HATTIC STATUETTE OF A WOMAN. SILVER, WITH GOLD-PLATED HEAD AND NECK. FROM HASANOĞLAN, NEAR ANKARA.
ABOUT 2000 B.C. HEIGHT 9½″. ARCHAEOLOGICAL MUSEUM, ANKARA.

bracelets, are a charming ornamental detail. Other decorative elements, such as the slight bulges formed by the breasts, navel and knees, the dotted pubic triangle, the anklets and the minutely carved toes, form with the rippling hair a splendid contrast to the finely polished surface of the body. The primitive forms and naive expression are charmingly mitigated by the precise drawing of the details and the excellence of the technical execution. The respectful pose of the hands leads one to see in the statuette a worshipper, perhaps a dead Hatti princess. The circumstances of the discovery, as reported by the peasants, and the other objects found with it prove that the precious figurine came from a tomb. The progressive outlook of the artist, who succeeded in his endeavor to model bodily forms naturalistically, indicates that the statuette is later than the small idols from the tombs at Alaca Höyük. It may well date from about 2000 B.C.

The royal tombs at Alaca Höyük and those recently discovered at Mahmutlar and Horoztepe have yielded a quantity of magnificent works of art that are unquestionably the finest products of prehistoric times. These precious treasure troves in gold, silver and bronze prove that in central Anatolia the last quarter of the third millennium marked the heyday of a unitary culture of a very high standard that had not yet invented writing but played a leading part in the mining and processing of precious metals. One is astonished to find that many swords had iron blades.

So against the dim background of the prehistoric age in Anatolia we get fascinating glimpses of a people who, though their language and religion are all but lost to us, reveal themselves in a great abundance of artifacts and works of art. Their name fortunately has been handed down: they called themselves Hatti, and for over fifteen hundred years Asia Minor was known as the Land of Hatti.

★

The story of another magnificent Bronze Age civilization is mirrored in the ruins of the citadel at Troy, whose discovery and excavation may well be termed one of the most significant scientific achievements of archaeological research.

Troy was excavated by Schliemann, Dörpfeld and Blegen. Schliemann was obsessed by the idea of discovering Priam's citadel and the scene of the Homeric poems. He began digging in 1870. When his great "north trench," which had become a byword, hit at a depth of 33 feet upon signs of a conflagration at the level of the second building period, he was convinced that he had found the traces of the Trojan War. So he took the treasure he discovered in that level for the "Treasure of Priam." The exploration of Troy took a lucky turn in 1882 when Schliemann obtained the assistance of the architect Wilhelm Dörpfeld, who since 1877 had belonged to the team that was excavating Olympia and gained great experience there. Dörpfeld distinguished nine building periods. This classification was confirmed and utilized by the American diggers who carried out new excavations at Troy under Carl W. Blegen from 1932 to 1938. The Americans brought to their work a greater degree of specialization thanks to the immense strides archaeology had made in the meantime, and their detailed observations enabled them to subdivide Dörpfeld's nine building periods into no less than thirty occupation levels.

The first monumental edifices erected in Anatolia with an eye to artistic town planning belong to the Trojan building phase. Although the unwalled city was just slightly over 110 yards in diameter—the citadel of Troy I measured only 100 yards across—the great *megaron* was a huge building located in the center of the citadel and at its highest point. It was some 150 feet long overall and 43 feet broad. The five-feet thick walls lead us to infer that its high flat roof dominated the fortifications and could be seen towering above them from a distance. It was surrounded by other *megara*. The whole complex gives an impression of regality. To enter the citadel one passed through the Main Gate and then through the Courtyard Gate. The two stately gate houses derived their shape from the *megaron*. Troy II is a development of the first settlement.

As in Troy I, the essential traits of the new period are early Aegean and early Cycladic. Blegen rightly insisted on the western character of that civilization. Imports of early Helladic "Urfirnis" pottery already found in the higher levels of Troy I continued, but it was now also copied in local workshops.

We can trace many contacts with the inland centers of Asia Minor and the East. Friedrich Matz rightly says that the rulers of Troy were not peasant kings but took advantage of their control over the international trade routes to assert their power and extend their domains. All metals—gold, silver, copper and tin—must have been imported from the central and eastern cities of Anatolia and from the East. Trojan artists learned the granulation process, an advanced goldsmiths' technique, and various methods of metal-working from eastern jewellers, who had been working precious metals for half a millennium. Their hoop-shaped earrings derive from an ancient eastern model. The finest examples of Trojan goldsmiths' work come from a treasure trove discovered by Schliemann; when the danger signal was given some forty centuries earlier it had been hidden in a hollow in the citadel wall. Besides a number of bronze vessels and weapons, the hoard comprises heavy drinking cups in gold and silver as well as gold articles of jewelry and silver bars. These latter must have been used for barter.

I would mention a gold vessel called the Sauceboat, which is 3 inches high and weighs 600 grams. Its shape is Aegean and the twin loop handles are strongly reminiscent of the *depas*, which is the typical Trojan vessel. The two beakshaped spouts are identical with those of the extremely elegant early Helladic long-spouted cups of the same period, which are made of clay coated with a glaze known as "Urfirnis."

The potters of Troy II were familiar with the two major technical innovations of their day—the kiln and the wheel. In the first Trojan settlement clay vessels were molded by hand and fired in an open hearth. The favorite shapes were two-handled cups, long-spouted jugs and face urns. It is clear to see that contacts with inland Asia Minor existed during both the first and second Trojan periods.

The second Trojan citadel suffered a dreadful catastrophe between 2200 and 2100 B.C.; the destruction of the fortress may perhaps be linked with the first inroads of the Indo-European tribes that reached Asia Minor just at that time. No traces of a new population have been found, however, in the following, insignificant building periods III, IV and V, which still belong to the early Bronze Age. And no cultural change seems to have occurred until the new settlement of Troy VI was established about 1800 B.C.

THE EARLY HITTITE PERIOD

The arrival of the Indo-European tribes in Asia Minor towards the end of the second millennium brought the grandiose development of the Hattic culture to a stop at least for a few centuries. We shall now see that this pause found an exact parallel in the northwestern corner of Anatolia, where the heyday of the second Trojan settlement was followed by the insignificant period of building phases III, IV and V. This simultaneous interruption of development in both parts of the peninsula leads us to view their impoverishment as the result of the disorder that may well have followed upon the Indo-European immigration.

We know of five city states in the Anatolian plateau that, during the first quarter of the eighteenth century, were ruled by petty kings. They are Kanesh (Nesa), Kussara, Hattusas, Zalpa and Puruskhanda. At the start, like many other cities not yet known to us by name, they were presumably all native principalities, in other words Hattic city states. As a result of the Indo-European immigration they fell into the hands of Hittite rulers.

To begin with, the most important of these cities was Kanesh, which is identical with the present-day Kültepe in the vicinity of Kayseri. Excavations carried out under the leadership of Tahsin and Nimet Özgüç, with Kemal Balkan in charge of philological research, have yielded some excellent finds. It is at Kültepe that we can discern the first traces of the Hittites, whose presence there was demonstrated by Sedat Alp. He made it clear that in the native proper names cited in texts found at Kültepe the terminations *ala*, *ili* and *ula* are Hittite modifications of the Hattic suffixes *al*, *il* and *ul*. Moreover, following in the footsteps of H. G. Güterbock, he has virtually proved, with new arguments, that Kanesh is identical with Nesa. The Hittites called themselves Nesians, so their capital must have been Nesa, nowadays known as Kültepe.

Writing was first employed in Anatolia in the days of the city states. Thousands of tablets inscribed in Assyrian cuneiform characters, containing information on many questions of interest at that period, have been found in the buried archives of the Assyrian merchant colony of Kültepe. The first Hittite rulers, for instance Anitta, King of Kussara, also seem to have employed Assyrian cuneiform script in the eighteenth century B.C. The unparalleled art of the Hittites developed from the harmonious interaction and reciprocal influence of the cultures of the Indo-European immigrants and the indigenous Hatti. The conquerors respected to a great extent the religion and customs of the native population and adapted themselves to local conditions. Their adoption of Hattic place and proper names is clear proof that the two ethnic elements became intimately blended.

EARLY HITTITE JUG WITH LONG SPOUT. CLAY WITH REDDISH BROWN GLAZE. FROM KÜLTEPE, 18TH CENTURY B.C. HEIGHT 15½".
ARCHAEOLOGICAL MUSEUM, ANKARA.

The high artistic level attained during the protohistoric period is most clearly seen in the monochrome pottery that embodies the indigenous component of the new development. Characteristic of the period is a type of long-spouted jug in which the angular, underslung girth and the sharp contours of the various parts make a charming contrast with the handsomely elongated spout. The burnished, red-brown surface sets off the severely simple forms. The arched handle and the upstretched spout display a balanced dynamism and a fascinating beauty. The two angular lugs on the shoulder and the elegant projection under the tip of the spout are more than mere ornaments, however effective: they perform a practical function as well. The projection is a drip-catcher and the two lugs enable the jug to be supported with one hand when pouring while the other hand grips the handle. The high polish aims at achieving the effect of a metal vessel and the tectonic structure also suggests a metallic prototype. This jug is the climax of a long evolution, the classic embodiment of a typical concept. There followed no further development, only imitation and—finally—decadence. Angular lines and sharp contours of the same kind, as well as boldly jutting spouts, appear in other types of vessels of the same period. They are characteristic traits that potters still clung to during the ensuing period of the Old Hittite Kingdom. Recent Turkish excavations at Kültepe and Karahöyük near Konya have also revealed the impressive remains of palaces and temples dating to the early Hittite period.

THE OLD HITTITE KINGDOM

The leading role in the shaping of the new Hattic-Indo-European civilization in Anatolia was played by the Nesians—namely the people who spoke Nesian and whom we nowadays call Hittites. From the very beginning the newly established state was so strong that only a few generations after it was founded, Mursilis I (c. 1620-1590 B.C.) conquered first Aleppo and then Babylon, thus bringing down the Hammurabi dynasty. The Hittites employed a cuneiform script imported from Mesopotamia during the eighteenth and seventeenth centuries. They also had a hieroglyphic script, which is found on seals and inscriptions on public monuments and recalls the hieroglyphs of Crete.

The art of the Old Hittite Kingdom is closely related to that of the previous period. The same burnished monochrome ware of tectonic design with handsome jutting spouts have been found at Alaca. But the slender lines of some types of vessels from Alaca, Alishar and Acem Höyük reflect a new artistic sensibility. The high standard of living in the Old Hittite Kingdom is demonstrated by the handsome earthenware hip-baths found in large numbers at Alishar and Boğazköy. The rather abstract figures of lions and bulls of the protohistoric period now assume naturalistic traits. A lion's head from Alishar, formerly on a rhyton, already presents the type of the stone lions that occur later during the Empire. Under the Old Kingdom Hittite builders continued in the tradition of the indigenous Anatolian architecture, but added unmistakably new technical and formal features. Typical is the Cyclopean wall that was not previously known in Anatolia. The palaces in the Hittite citadel of Hattusas, where the rulers of the Old Kingdom lived, must have been identical with those of the foregoing early Hittite period that have recently come to light. The most recent German excavations at Boğazköy (the modern Turkish name of ancient Hattusas) have proved that the underground posterns used for offensive defense during the Empire were also known in the days of the Old Kingdom.

THE HITTITE EMPIRE

In the fifteenth and fourteenth centuries the Hittites were one of the three most important states in the Near East and in the thirteenth they shared power over the entire world of their day with the Egyptians. The singular civilization they created was of a very high order.

Hittite art enjoyed its heyday during the Empire. That period witnessed the first development of their monumental architecture and colossal sculpture. The erection of grand temples and palaces led to the creation of a visual art that attained an eminent place in the eastern world. The Hittites were the best military architects of their day. The offensive defenses they raised during the Old Kingdom developed under the Empire into fortifications that are quite unique. The impressive Cyclopean walls of Hattusas and Alaca are technically beyond reproach. The city walls of ancient Hattusas have never been equalled in the strategic adaptation of their design to the extremely difficult terrain and in the layout of their offensive defenses.

The German excavations of Hattusas (Boğazköy) brought to light five temples whose size and structure place them among the grandest monuments of the second millennium in the whole known world of that day. The largest, which is dedicated to the local weather god, is very well preserved and still gives a very good idea of what it looked like at the time. The whole complex, storerooms included, is about 530 feet long by 450 feet wide. The temple proper comprises a rectangular edifice with inner courtyard and an annex containing the actual shrines. The statue of the deity, unfortunately no longer extant, was exposed to view in the largest of the nine chambers in the annex.

The major characteristic of Hittite architecture is the totally asymmetrical ground-plan. The column was unknown to the Hittites, who used square piers as supporting members. Nor did they know the capital. Typical, indeed unique, features are the large windows with low parapets cut in the outer walls of the temples instead of facing the courtyard. The section of the chamber in which the image of the god used to be exposed, projects, so that the idol was illumined from three sides. This fondness for light might indicate that the Hittites originally worshipped in the open air—a custom still preserved in the sanctuary at Yazılıkaya.

Unfortunately not one of the idols from their temples has been preserved. Indeed, we have no monumental sculpture in the round dating from the Hittite Empire. However, a large number of very handsome reliefs are still extant. The most important are carved in the rock faces at the sanctuary of Yazılıkaya not far northeast of Hattusas. The large gallery with reliefs of male and female deities used to be the cella of the temple that preceded it and whose foundations have been laid bare. The rites, which at Hattusas were performed in closed chambers before the cult statue, took place here in the open air before reliefs representing the entire Hittite pantheon.

The side gallery was reserved for the sovereign's own devotions. On its north side there was once the statue of the great king Tudhalyas IV; the pedestal is still preserved, as is the cartouche in relief on the wall. The other reliefs in this gallery represent King Tudhalyas in the embrace of the god Sharruma, the sword god, and a procession of twelve gods. All these reliefs, as well as the mountain god on the king's cartouche, face north, that is, towards the statue. Whoever entered the side gallery through the south door (now inaccessible) saw the statue of the ruler in front of him, exposed to view in a dominating position before the north wall.

The significance of the sword god has not yet been explained. He must be viewed as a genuine deity on account of the many horns and divine ideograms that adorn the inside of his conical hat. But we do not yet know enough about Hittite religion and mythology to solve the riddle. There is also a possibility that the image may not have any religious connotation. For in reality it is merely a minor-art motif blown up to a monumental scale. It may be simply a sculptured reproduction of a certain sword that belonged to the royal family. Many examples of sword-hilts similarly embellished with lions' heads have been discovered in the East. Tudhalyas IV may have owned a very precious weapon that was depicted here in his chamber as a symbol of his power.

The lions on the Lion Gate at Boğazköy (Hattusas) and the sphinxes at Alaca Höyük can still be seen *in situ*. One of the sphinxes from the Sphinx Gate at Boğazköy is preserved in Berlin, the other in Istanbul. The gate god from the King's Gate at Boğazköy is now in the Ankara Museum together with all the orthostats from the walls of Alaca.

PROCESSION OF TWELVE HITTITE GODS IN THE GUISE OF ARMED WARRIORS. ROCK RELIEF AT YAZILIKAYA, SECOND HALF OF THE 13TH CENTURY B.C. HEIGHT OF THE FIGURES 31½″.

The iconographic details of the Hittite reliefs show that they were made by sculptors who worked to fixed formulas and precepts. Not only the various parts of the head-dress, hair-style and costume, but even the limbs were always represented in accordance with a rigid convention. The facial features—eyes, brows, mouth and ears—were drawn to a standard pattern. A characteristic of the Hittite male type is that he always wears a ring, sometimes a beard, but never a moustache. The posture of the arms, whether or not there is something in the hand, is always the same. In the male figures the near arm (as seen by the spectator) is sharply bent and pressed against the body, while the other is only slightly bent and rather outstretched. In the female figures both arms are bent forwards.

During the Empire pottery was very unimportant compared with sculpture. Some pieces still extant prove that a polychrome style had been brought to perfection. A good example of this sort of courtly art is a very fine vessel from Bitik decorated with figures in relief whose faces closely resemble those on the reliefs from Alaca Höyük. This handsome work dates from about 1400 B.C.

The second German excavations at Boğazköy that started in 1931 under Kurt Bittel and were resumed under the same successful leadership after the Second World War yielded at each campaign new works of art of the highest quality and significance. Thus operations in the citadel (Böyük Kale) in 1963 brought to light two magnificent clay bulls that I should like to describe briefly here.

THE HITTITE SWORD GOD. ROCK RELIEF AT YAZILIKAYA, SECOND HALF OF THE 13TH CENTURY B.C.
HEIGHT OF THE FIGURE 10½ FEET.

Nearly four feet high, the two Boğazköy bulls are ritual vessels used for libations on certain occasions. "Their use is explained by a funnel-shaped input aperture at the point where the neck joins the back and two outlet holes in the nostrils," says Peter Neve, who published the precious objects. "One is struck by the fact that the two bulls are identical except that the tip of the tail is attached to the left hind leg in one and to the right hind leg in the other. This difference proves that the bulls formed a pair, symbolizing maybe the yoke of sacred bulls Seri and Hurri." They belonged to the weather god and are depicted in the main scene at Yazılıkaya and on the great relief at Malatya, where they draw the god's chariot. We can also see them harnessed to the god's chariot from Imamkulu. The diggers were quick to observe that every slightest fragment of the two bulls had been carefully hidden in the earth. Neve says: "One might surmise that the vessels were damaged through long service and gradually became useless. However, being ritual instruments, they could not be simply discarded but had to be buried with solemn ceremony." He rightly suggests that the bulls were made during the early Empire period.

Other important states existed in Anatolia at the time of the Hittites. The Mitanni kingdom, most powerful of the Hurrian lands, lay to the east and southeast; it played an important role about the middle of the second millennium. Hurrian is one of the strangest languages in the eastern world—very different from those of the Semitic and Indo-European groups, very different too from the prefixing Hattic—and has an agglutinative character. The Hurrian civilization exerted a great influence on the religion and literature of the Hittites. At the time of the Empire the peoples of Asia Minor had adopted the Hurrian pantheon. We can see their deities portrayed on the reliefs of the rock sanctuary at Yazılıkaya. The Gilgamesh epic, the myths of Kumarbi and the horse trainer Kikkuli's work are based on original Hurrian texts. The Hurrian civilization reveals in turn Indo-Aryan and Luwian influences. All the Mitanni kings had Indian names, which means that the Hurrians were governed by an aristocracy of Indo-Aryan origin. That noble caste, which was apparently very thin on the ground, was constituted by the knights who bred horses and fought on chariots; they were called Marianni and were certainly responsible for the spread of horse breeding and the use of war chariots through the Near East.

At the present stage of research the only Hurrian arts we know of are cylinder seals and pottery. The most characteristic motifs on seals are hybrid beings, the pillars of heaven and the sacred tree. Some seals reveal Cretan and Mycenaean influences, as can be seen in representations of chariots and winged horses. Typically Hurrian are the large cup-shaped vessels with decorative ornaments on a black ground. This type of pottery first appears in the reign of Shaushattar, in the middle of the fifteenth century, and continues in more highly developed examples at Alalakh. The mural paintings from Nuzi portraying cows' heads viewed from the front and women's heads with cows' ears should also be considered as products of Mitannian art.

HITTITE RITUAL VESSELS IN THE FORM OF BULLS. CLAY. FROM BOĞAZKÖY,
14TH CENTURY B.C. HEIGHT 35½″. ARCHAEOLOGICAL MUSEUM, ANKARA.

The Luwians were Indo-Europeans who lived in the southern part of the Anatolian peninsula, but all we know of them today is their language. This is also true of the Palaians, another Indo-European people, whose traces are found in the region of Paphlagonia. No cultural legacies of Arzawa, Kizzuwadna or Assuwa, situated in the south or west of the peninsula, have yet been discovered or recognized. A state called Ahhiyawâ mentioned in Hittite texts lay presumably in southwestern Asia Minor.

The middle Bronze Age settlement of Troy VI, which replaced the early Bronze Age civilization in the same locality, was founded about the time when the Indo-European immigrants set up their first city states on the plateau. It was probably no mere chance that in Greece the early Bronze Age came to an end and the middle Bronze Age began at that very time. The rise of these new contemporary civilizations in three neighboring parts of the ancient world may well be due to the great Indo-European immigration that started towards the end of the third millennium and probably continued until the beginning of the second. Blegen has clearly proved that the inhabitants of Troy VI were originally related to those of the middle Helladic cities on the Greek mainland. We can distinguish a similar, though far less obvious affinity of the same origin between the Hittite civilization and that of Troy VI. Although from the start the Hittites felt a very strong eastern influence, yet, as I have already pointed out in another place, they reveal a certain essential kinship with Mycenae and Troy VI particularly as regards architecture and town planning.

However, the contact between Troy and Hattusas seems to have been very lax. Not even the smallest Hittite sherd has ever been discovered at Troy. The only object that might have come from the land of the Hittites is a spear tip that naturally does not tell us much. The similar traits that can be observed in the architecture and pottery of the two centers do not point to a direct contact between them but should rather be ascribed to native Anatolian influences that reached Troy by devious routes. The overland route was unsafe and both traditional relations and the geopolitical situation linked Troy with the West. Imported pottery includes mat painted ware of Helladic and Cycladic origin and Mycenaean ware. Cretan works of art and fragments of Cypriot pottery discovered there confirm that Troy VI maintained its relations with the outer world by the sea route. Its finest products are the Minyan ware found in large quantities in the earlier occupation levels of the sixth settlement. This technique the Trojans, like their contemporaries on the Greek mainland, had brought with them from their common fatherland.

The citadel of Troy VI was undoubtedly one of the finest fortresses of its time. The impressive remains of the city wall 10 to 13 feet high give us a good idea of its original appearance. It was presumably erected at the turn of the fifteenth century. The flat bastions, which result in a jagged ground-plan, are, as Rudolf Naumann demonstrated at Alishar, an architectural feature indigenous to Anatolia. Inside the citadel were handsome *megara*, the majestic palaces of the Trojan princes. The site was terraced in concentric semicircles. Actually, only the buildings on the southern half of the lower terraces have come down to us. The houses and palaces on the higher parts of the citadel were sacrificed by the planners in Hellenistic-Roman times. A half-annular terraced plan of the same type can be observed in the citadel of Hattusas and the acropolis of Pergamum. The strict separation of the various buildings is another planning principle common to the citadels of Troy VI and Hattusas. It later became one of the absolute principles of Greek urban architecture.

The highest occupation level of the sixth citadel, which Blegen dates about 1325-1275 B.C., is Homer's Troy. The Trojan War was due to the city's vital strategic position and the economic ambitions of the Mycenaeans. The Iliad may be the story of the unsuccessful attacks launched by the Achaeans against Troy VI. The impregnable fortress was only conquered by the stratagem of the wooden horse, as related in the Odyssey. This mythical detail of the epic is the real proof that the Trojan War was a historical fact. Poets do not lack imagination, but how could Homer or his predecessors have hit upon the story of the wooden horse if the Achaeans had not actually set up the image of a horse in Troy to express their gratitude to Poseidon, the Earth Shaker, for having destroyed the mighty citadel that they had been unable to take? Today we know, thanks to Blegen's subtle observations, that Troy was first wrecked by a violent earthquake in 1275 and only in 1240 fell into the hands of the Achaeans. But no one can say for sure that the authors of the epics were aware of that natural phenomenon. In fact there is no hint or reference to any such thing in the poems. Therefore the motif of the wooden horse is the historical core of the saga. And victory only smiled on the attackers after the city had suffered the tremendous catastrophe. Hardly had the Trojans repaired the walls, restored some of the old buildings and built some new homes, when the cunning, ruthless Achaeans came and set fire to the city.

The defeat suffered by the Trojans at the hands of their inimical kinsmen brought to a sad end a power that had been the bulwark of Anatolia against the West. Soon the city fell into the hands of the Thracians (Troy VII b2), who had long wanted to obtain possession of the fertile lands of northwestern Asia Minor and now, about 1180 B.C., attacked the Hittite Empire in mighty waves.

THE COMING OF THE THRACIANS
AND ANATOLIA'S DARK AGE

The presence of the Thracians in Troy VII b2 since about 1200 B.C. is proved by the finding in that level of large quantities of "Buchelkeramik," which is known as the characteristic pottery of the Eastern European peoples. At Hattusas written sources disappear about 1180. That date too confirms the assumption that Hattusas was conquered by Thracian tribes. A most important document for the immigration of the Southeastern Europeans into Asia Minor is the Annals of the Assyrian king Tiglath-Pileser I, who reigned from 1112 to 1074. They tell us that he waged war on the Mushki, who had appeared on the northeast frontier of Assyria on the upper reaches of the Tigris fifty years before his accession. So these Mushki—perhaps they are to be identified with the Moesians of Southeast Europe—and presumably many other Balkan tribes had stood at the gates of Assyria since about 1170 after overrunning Troy and Hattusas.

Egyptian sources too are in complete agreement with these dates. Ramses III (1200-1168) calls "Sea or Island Peoples" the tribes that had appeared on the frontiers and coasts of his empire; but since he also says that they had destroyed Arzawa, Carchemish and other cities, his words confirm the Assyrian annals. For Carchemish lies on the upper Euphrates not far from the frontier of the Assyrian empire of that time. We learn from the Egyptian sources that this huge migration did not involve solely the Thracian and Southeastern European tribes but that the Sea and Island peoples also took part. The Dorian migration that swept mainland Greece was a branch of the same human flood.

These ruthless aggressions had catastrophic consequences. The immigrants destroyed the civilized countries of Asia Minor so relentlessly and with such elemental fury that their coming was followed by a dark age that lasted two hundred years in Western Anatolia and no less than four hundred on the plateau. Years ago I pointed out that between 1180 and 775 B.C. central Anatolia was very thinly populated by nomadic tribes, so that we cannot expect to find any material traces of them in the occupation mounds. The catastrophe was so vast that even the Hittite tradition was totally lost in that region. One thing is certain: no urban settlements existed in the heart of the Hittite empire before the rise of the Phrygian state. Consequently, none of the present-day names of the towns in the center of Asia Minor, such as Gordion, Ankara, Yozgat, Çorum, Tokat, Boğazköy, Kırşehir, etc., is of Hittite origin, as is the case for the centers south of the Halys bend and the southern Anatolian towns of Niğde, Adana, Malatya, Marash and Carchemish, all of which date back to Hittite times if not to an even earlier period.

1545350

LATE HITTITE TOMBSTONE OF A MARRIED COUPLE. FROM MARASH, ABOUT 700 B.C. HEIGHT 39″.
ARCHAEOLOGICAL MUSEUM, ANKARA.

NEO-HITTITE ART

In southeastern Anatolia and northern Syria, where there seems to have been no dark age, the Neo-Hittite principalities developed a remarkable activity after the fall of the Empire. Neo-Hittite art reveals three clearly distinguishable styles, namely Old Neo-Hittite, Middle Neo-Hittite and Late Neo-Hittite.

The Old Neo-Hittite style (1200-900 B.C.) carries on the art of the Empire and is attested exclusively at Malatya. The great relief there, which I have already mentioned, is a typical example of this traditional style. It comprises two consecutive scenes. On the left we see the weather god on his chariot drawn by the two bulls, Seri and Hurri. On the right, after dismounting from the chariot, he receives the libation offered him by King Sulumeli; the god holds a boomerang in his right hand and brandishes a thunderbolt in his left. In the background on a level with his head, two hieroglyphs—the deity ideogram and the weather god symbol—designate him in two different ways as the weather god. Both stylistically and iconographically this relief is an offspring of the Yazılıkaya and Alaca schools of sculpture, which produced outstanding works of art under the Empire.

The Middle Neo-Hittite style (900-750 B.C.), unlike the foregoing, is not an immediate continuation of the Anatolian-Hittite tradition but, although the art of the Empire period was still thriving, reveals peculiar traits and elements all its own. Its best and most characteristic examples were unearthed at Carchemish and Zincirli. The finds from the former locality are kept in the Ankara Museum, those from the latter at Istanbul and Berlin.

The Late Neo-Hittite style (750-700 B.C.) presents two facets: Hittite-Assyrian and Hittite-Aramaic. The Araras reliefs from Carchemish belong to the former trend; the sculptures from Zincirli, Sakçegözü, Marash and Karatepe to the latter.

The stela from the tomb of a married couple at Marash is an outstanding work of art in the Late Neo-Hittite style. The two spouses face the beholder seated side by side with their feet resting on a footstool; they have their arms round each other's shoulders in an affectionate embrace. Their melancholy facial expressions show that they are dead. The husband's hair and beard are arranged in ringlets after the Assyrian fashion. The wife instead wears the same low, richly ornamented Hittite *polos* as the Middle Neo-Hittite *kupaba* from Carchemish and also the same girdle. The little cloak with its ends tucked into the girdle recalls sixth-century Ionian sculptures. The wife sits at her husband's left hand. This was an ancient Hittite custom which had been adopted in Anatolia since early Hittite times and became an absolute ceremonial rule,

LATE HITTITE SPHINX OF THE NORTH GATEWAY AT KARATEPE. ABOUT 700 B.C. IN SITU.

particularly under the Empire. The bunch of grapes in the man's hand symbolizes his calling: he may have been a wealthy wine merchant. The dead portrayed on other stelae from Marash hold various objects in their hands, such tools of their trade as a writing stylus and tablets or a weighing scales. Here the woman carries a mirror in her left hand, like the Hittite ladies of quality. On her gown is a Phrygian fibula—the peak of fashion in those days. Her ear ornaments are unusually rich: besides the drops hanging from the lobe, other pieces of jewelry made of pearls or precious stones encircle the shell. She also wears a nose-ring. Like the goddess from Tell Halaf, she wears several anklets. The man's robe has the same length as his wife's. It is the simple garment of the Middle Neo-Hittite period. His waistband, though uncommonly broad, is familiar to us from Middle Neo-Hittite works. Both figures wear sandals that leave the toes bare.

This gravestone, which is an extraordinarily expressive work, is one of the most significant artistic products of the ancient East. Except for the sphinx from Karatepe, it is the only eastern work in which the human face expresses a quite definite state of mind. It is true that the Assyrians depicted animals as suffering, enraged or roaring, with truly dramatic effect. But the faces of their human figures have a masklike fixity. The Aramaeans seem to have been the first people of historic times to portray human beings with menacing, gloomy and even joyful faces. The tombstone from Marash presumably dates from the end of the eighth century at the earliest.

The interesting sculptures discovered at Karatepe by H. T. Bossert and his team count among the latest examples of Hittite-Aramaic art. But they also reveal extensive Phoenician influences. Indeed, many of these works should be designated as "Phoenician-style" Hittite. The unusually lively portrayal of the sphinx from the North Gate is a typical example of this new trend. The fabulous monster's hair style, ethnical type, apron and epaulettes are directly inspired by the Phoenicians. The monster was entrusted, as an averter of evil, with the task of guarding the entrance to the palace. The sculptor succeeded in a masterly fashion in producing a mask whose staring, gem-studded eyes and pursed lips are truly terrifying.

Sculpture schools of outstanding artistic quality were active during the second half of the eighth century, particularly at Zincirli and Sakçegözü. The works produced in those localities made a very strong impact on Greek and Etruscan art. Greek representations of lions and griffins are particularly faithful copies of the ones produced in those centers, but Greek art felt the influence of Late Neo-Hittite art in many other ways. Thanks to the geographical position of the small principalities at the keypoints of the Near East and the favorable historical conditions that prevailed in the eighth century, the Hittites, Luwians and Aramaeans, who in peaceful coexistence had created a common civilization, came to be accepted by the Greeks as the worthy representatives of the eastern world.

URARTIAN ART

The Urartians, who descended from the Hurrians, founded in eastern Anatolia, on the plateau around Lake Van and in what is today the Armenian province of the USSR, an empire whose civilization was strongly influenced by the Assyrians. Their works of art were very popular in their day. In particular, bronze cauldrons adorned with human heads or the foreparts of animals were exported to Phrygia, Greece and Etruria.

A worthy representative of Urartian art is the bronze cauldron and relative tripod from Altıntepe near Erzincan preserved in the Ankara Museum. Its design may be viewed as typical of Urartu, for other cauldrons from that locality have similar forms. Peculiarly Urartian traits, as Pierre Amandry has pointed out, are the four bull's heads that adorn the rim and above all the slender, rhythmically curving horns that form plastic rings where they join the head. Other features of Urartian representations of bulls are the stylized curls of the forelock that covers part of the head like a rectangular piece of material; the frontlet that spans the forehead from ear to ear; and the wing-shaped plates on which the heads are mounted. Attempts at stylistic classification of the bull cauldron have so far proved abortive. The magnificent work may date from the end of the eighth century or more probably from the seventh.

We are learning more and more about the Urartian civilization. The Russian scholars Piotrovski and Oganesyan discovered Urartian building levels at Karmir Blur and Arin Berd that yielded outstanding works of art. Excavations at present under way on the sites of several Urartian cities, conducted by the Turkish philologists, historians and archaeologists Balkan, Bilgiç, Erzen, Özgüç and Temizer, have brought to light a quantity of new material of extraordinarily high quality.

PHRYGIAN ART

In central Asia Minor the Phrygians created a magnificent civilization that belongs chiefly to the Greek sphere but was strongly influenced by both Neo-Hittites and Urartians. The Phrygians were originally a Thracian tribe that probably had a hand in the destruction of Troy VIIa and Hattusas, but are not archaeologically attested until about the middle of the eighth century. The Phrygian empire was founded by Midas, but it was short-lived (c. 725-675 B.C.), falling a victim to the Cimmerian invasion in the first quarter of the seventh century.

URARTIAN CAULDRON WITH TRIPOD FROM ALTINTEPE, NEAR ERZINCAN. BRONZE.
8TH OR 7TH CENTURY B.C. HEIGHT OF CAULDRON 17¾". ARCHAEOLOGICAL MUSEUM, ANKARA.

The most important finds have come from Gordion, the Phrygian capital, and other centers of that civilization such as Alishar, Boğazköy, Alaca, Pazarlı and Ankara. The works of art from the German excavations carried out at Gordion at the beginning of the present century are preserved in the Museum at Istanbul. Those unearthed by the Americans, who have been digging at Gordion with great success for the last fifteen years under the leadership of Rodney S. Young, are kept in the Ankara Museum. The Phrygians developed a civilization of the highest order. Their script, which closely resembles the Greek, was already in use at the end of the eighth century if not earlier. Their eminent works of art exerted a strong influence even on Cycladic vase painting. Phrygian metal and textile products were very popular in the entire Greek world.

After the Cimmerian invasion the Phrygians enjoyed in the first half of the sixth century an Indian summer that reached its highest point in their new centers at Eskişehir and Afyon. The grandiose rock monuments there are very well preserved.

The noblest of these works is perhaps the one at Yazılıkaya, the so-called Tomb of Midas near Eskişehir. This monument, almost 60 feet high, is hewn in the living rock. In shape it resembles the façade of a building and provides an architectural frame for the niche in which the image of the goddess Cybele was exposed on festive occasions. The main feature of the Phrygian rock façades, which distinguishes them from all other rock monuments of that period in Asia Minor, is the geometric ornamentation. We find the same decorative idiom in contemporary terracotta friezes and on many other artistic monuments in wood, mosaic and clay. It is a national peculiarity and forms a charming contrast with the vast proportions of the towering structures. As a matter of fact, these Phrygian rock monuments give the impression of a rather forced grandeur and seem on the whole the result of the transposition of minor art forms on a colossal scale. But it cannot be denied that the outcome was a success.

The monument at Yazılıkaya has two inscriptions, one of which mentions the name of Midas. Herodotus tells us that several kings of Phrygia were called Gordios and Midas, so that is not a decisive factor in the dating of the monument. However, the other Phrygian rock façades in the same district can be ascribed to the middle or third quarter of the sixth century on account of their reliefs, which reveal a strong Greek influence. Consequently, the monument at Yazılıkaya, which has the same type of façade, cannot have been cut before the beginning of that century.

THE LYCIAN, LYDIAN AND CARIAN CIVILIZATIONS

The same period saw the heyday to the west of the Anatolian plateau of the important civilizations of the Lycians, Lydians and Carians, all of whom may be considered as indigenous peoples of that country. Like Hittite, the languages of the Lydians and Lycians belong to the Indo-European-Anatolian group, but they contain many relics of pre-Indo-European tongues. Consequently, the Lycians and Lydians represent, at least in part, the ancient pre-Hittite cultures of Anatolia, whose true heirs presumably still survived in the first half of the first millennium B.C., though they have not yet been archaeologically attested.

Xanthos, the capital of Lycia, is one of the finest ruined cities in Anatolia and offers for our admiration not only fascinating Lycian monuments dating from the sixth to the third centuries B.C. in an excellent state of preservation but also the well preserved remains of Roman buildings. The French excavations made on that site in recent years under the direction of Pierre Demargne have brought to light grandiose works of art that are now kept in the Istanbul Museum. At Sardis, one-time capital of the Lydian empire that was so greatly admired by the Greeks, systematic digging started in 1958 under George M. A. Hanfmann has also achieved extraordinarily important results.

The Carians used a script similar to those of the Lydians, Phrygians, Lycians and Greeks, but it has proved undecipherable up to the present day. So we cannot say to what language group Carian belongs. Herodotus relates that, according to a Cretan tradition, the Carians were called Lelegians and lived on the islands in Minoan times. But the Carians themselves did not agree: they claimed to be natives of Anatolia and kinsmen of the Lydians and Mysians.

Italian excavations in the past and those now in course under the direction of Doro Levi in the Carian region have produced remarkable results. The finds from the new Italian diggings at Iasos are kept in the museum at Smyrna. The more ancient works of art unearthed by the Swedish expedition mentioned below on the site of the Carian city of Labranda are to be found in the same museum.

The western and central Anatolian civilizations dealt with briefly above had been influenced by the Greek populations of West Anatolia since 650 B.C. at least. This Greek influence is still more patent from the sixth century on. Nonetheless, those civilizations managed to preserve their own character up to the days of Alexander the Great. Only after 300 B.C. did Greek art dominate the whole of Anatolia. At the time artists in the entire peninsula still relied for their subjects and motifs on the ancient Anatolian tradition that lived on as a happy blend until the spread of Christianity.

PHRYGIAN CULT MONUMENT KNOWN AS THE TOMB OF MIDAS. AT YAZILIKAYA, NEAR ESKIŞEHIR, FIRST HALF OF THE 6TH CENTURY B.C. HEIGHT ABOUT 60 FEET.

ARCHAIC IONIAN HEAD FROM A STATUE AT SAMOS. MARBLE. ABOUT 550 B.C. HEIGHT 18½″. ARCHAEOLOGICAL MUSEUM, ISTANBUL.

THE AGE OF THE ANATOLIAN GREEK CIVILIZATION

The most recent excavations of ancient Smyrna and Miletus have made it clear that the Aeolian and Ionian cities on the west coast of Asia Minor were founded about 1000 B.C. The new material at hand today enables us to form an idea of the true role played by East Greek art in the Hellenic world.

The early Greek colonies in Anatolia started out as paltry, primitive settlements. During the first centuries—from 1050 to 750 B.C.—the Greek immigrants lived chiefly by agriculture. Their houses consisted of a single room and were built in a primitive fashion. In the matter of art they were entirely under the influence of the mother country. Though their proto-geometric and geometric pottery was a local product, yet in both style and technique it slavishly copied Greek prototypes.

The upsurge first started in the Ionian cities. Panionion, the Ionian League, whose capital was located close to the coast at the foot of the Mycale mountain range, was founded probably as early as the ninth century to assist their expansion against the Aeolian cities. This political federation may have enabled the Ionians to expand as far as Northwest Asia Minor. Sherds found in the Milesian colony of Cyzicus (Kyzikos) prove that it was established at the beginning of the seventh century.

In those early days the East Greek world experienced its first cultural advance. The mother country had a long start in the fields of art and economics, but the Greeks of Asia Minor were the spiritual leaders. The founding of their oldest cities and the creation of the Homeric poems gave the Ionians first place in the Hellenic world, and as regards social development and intellectual pursuits they kept that place during the period that ensued.

But the true heyday of the East Greek world only came when the Milesians started to colonize the Mediterranean and Black Sea coasts of Asia Minor about the middle of the seventh century B.C. The stimulus of trade and industry, and the wealth these brought in their wake, resulted in a prosperity that developed on Anatolian soil in the course of the sixth century.

Aeolian-Ionian art and culture owe their originality largely to the lengthy contact with the Lydian, Lycian, Carian and other indigenous Anatolian cultures. The Phrygians should also be mentioned in this context for, though descended from Thracian settlers, they became so thoroughly assimilated to the native Anatolians that by the beginning of the sixth century they had developed into a genuine people of Asia Minor.

The coexistence of the Greek colonists and the indigenous population gave rise to the Ionian civilization that not only produced in the sixth century, with the help of manifold eastern influences, a magnificent literature and a unique art but also, by laying the foundations of the exact sciences, brought forth the first fruits of western thought. The first half of the sixth century witnessed the rise of Ionian architecture and sculpture. Then the outstanding works of Ionian artists and Aeolian-Ionian poets placed the mother country under their spell. The novel elements in Attic sculpture—the chiton, the small diagonal cloak, the rendering of drapery, and the radiant, joyous facial expression—are characteristic traits of Ionian art.

The major centers of the Ionian school of sculpture were Miletus and Samos. At the start Samian artists followed the lead given by the Cycladic and Attic workshops, but towards the middle of the sixth century works in the Ionian taste were produced on the island. A splendid head in Istanbul Museum belonging to a body discovered a few years ago on Samos may be viewed as a masterpiece of this new trend. In style it is half way between the Ephesian Girl, a reliefed column, and the Youth's Head from Hieronda. As in the Ephesian Girl, the smooth planes of the face make a fine contrast with the disordered hair. But the voluptuous forms bring it closer to the Youth from Hieronda. The masterly modelling of the features, which results in a fascinating play of light and shade, produces a painterly effect like that of a head found near the Temple of Artemis. The deep-set eyes and delicately modelled lips give the face a delightful expression, but on the whole it is the head of a self-reliant leader, a prince, "perhaps even a tyrant." It dates presumably from about the middle of the sixth century.

One of the finest pieces of Ionian sculpture so far discovered is the head of a girl from a carved column of the Temple of Apollo at Didyma. The face is broad and round, with sharply chiselled lips and eyelids. The eyebrows continue the curve of the nose without a break, forming a graceful arch over the nose. The wide, thin-lipped mouth repeats the effect of the slotted eyes. The bland smile playing on the lips strengthens the expression of the joy-filled eyes. Something of their blithe animation is even communicated to the cheeks. This face conveys unforgettably the charm of the Ionian spirit and stands out as one of the most fascinating works of art to come down to us from the ancient world. It can be dated to about the middle of the sixth century.

The Ionians made a far greater and more important contribution to architecture than to sculpture. The elegance, charm and originality of Greek architecture is largely due to the creative power and artistic sensibility of the Ionian mind. The slender proportions of Ionic forms mitigated the ponderous solidity that Greek architecture owed to the Doric order, and so gave it greater variety and ensured its future. In the classical period, when the grave Doric style, which had already become the canon, needed enrichment it found it in the Ionic elements to which the monuments on the Acropolis of Athens owe their serene, joyful vitality.

IONIAN HEAD OF A GIRL FROM THE TEMPLE OF APOLLO AT DIDYMA. MARBLE. ABOUT 550 B.C. HEIGHT 22″. STAATLICHE MUSEEN, BERLIN.

IONIAN PAINTED VASE FROM THE NECROPOLIS AT ÇANDARLI (PITANE). ABOUT 560 B.C. HEIGHT 15¾".
ARCHAEOLOGICAL MUSEUM, ISTANBUL.

Unfortunately the only remnants of the grand buildings erected by the Ionians in the sixth century are fragments preserved in London and Berlin as well as in the Turkish museums of Istanbul, Izmir and Ephesus. We can obtain some idea of what they looked like from the well preserved Ionic temples at Didyma, Sardis and Aizani, though they date from a far later period. The finest Anatolian-Ionian sculptures of the sixth century are to be found in museums in Berlin, London, Istanbul and Izmir.

In the domain of vase painting, instead, that period was a time of stagnation for East Greek art. When the Athenian painters produced their important and novel vases with black figures at the beginning of the sixth century, the workshops in the East Greek centers remained true to the traditional Orientalizing style. In the necropolis at Çandarlı (Pitane) we have brought to light vases that date from the second quarter of the sixth century but are painted in the recessed technique of the seventh.

The early Greek period in Anatolia, succinctly described above, has mostly been studied during the last few decades. The eminent scholars Carl Weickert, Karl Schefold, John M. Cook, Gerhard Kleiner, Pierre Devambez and Henri Metzger have conducted excavations in western Asia Minor and made valuable contributions to our knowlege of the period. The author of these lines has participated in this research with his excavations of some early Greek cities in Anatolia. A number of diggings are still in active progress.

For two centuries, from the conquest of the Lydian empire by Cyrus (546 B.C.), to the crossing of the Dardanelles by Alexander the Great (334 B.C.), Anatolia was dominated by the Persians. A number of Persian and Greco-Persian works of art found in Pontus, Cappadocia, Lycia and in the Propontis date from that period. Several sculptures in the Greco-Persian style have come to light in the region of Lake Manyas in north-western Asia Minor and above all in the locality called Ergili, which not so long ago we identified with the ancient Dascylium, capital of the Persian satrapy of Propontis.

Like most of the East Greek towns Pitane was in its prime from about 625 to 545 B.C. Our excavations in the cemetery, carried out over the past five years, have brought to light some fine pottery dating to this period, mostly Chian ware. Over thirty complete painted vases of this ware have so far been found. Two of them, both over fifteen inches high, have figure paintings which show us what the archaic wall paintings of about 560 B.C. must have been like: one depicts a scene of leave-taking between a warrior and seven horsemen; the other, Achilles ambushing and slaying the Trojan prince Troilus.

The different workshops of the Orientalizing style of vase painting are abundantly represented. Most numerous are the painted vases of a local workshop, situated either at Myrina or at Pitane itself, whose products have great charm and beauty. Among the pieces of Attic pottery are two bowls decorated by the Heidelberg Master. The finds from the Pitane excavations are exhibited partly in the Izmir (Smyrna) Museum, partly in the Archaeological Museum, Istanbul.

GRECO-PERSIAN STELA FROM ERGILI (DASCYLIUM). MARBLE.
ABOUT 400 B.C. HEIGHT 87″. ARCHAEOLOGICAL MUSEUM, ISTANBUL.

The finest works of this type, after the well-known women on horseback from Ergili, are perhaps the three sculptured stelae recently found in the same neighborhood and published in a learned article by Necati Dolunay. Here is a brief description of the best preserved of the three.

This stela, as we can see from one of the others, was formerly crowned with a palmette acroterium. The molding at the top consists of a broad fillet and an Ionic cymatium of the type found on the funerary stelae of the fifth and fourth centuries; the same molding is repeated at the foot. But these three stelae are not tombstones. The one with the palmette acroterium bears an inscription in Aramaic which, as read by A. Dupont-Sommer, tells us that an Aramaic or Phoenician caravan owner, Elnaf, son of Ishai, a votary of the gods Baal and Nabu, erected it (and probably the one reproduced here as well) in order that the caravan might have a prosperous journey and nothing untoward happen to any of its members.

The Elnaf mentioned in the inscription was presumably the model for the male figure sitting on the couch in the banquet scene. He may very well be the rider on the stela with the palmette acroterium too.

The figured relief displays in form and content a blend of Greek and Persian elements, which I shall now try to identify in detail. The wheeled container, which occurs in very similar shape on the attic of the Sarcophagus with the Weeping Women at Istanbul, is probably Persian because the container of another wagon on that work is an exact copy of a Persian model. Moreover, the big, eight-spoked wheel reinforced with iron nails occurs on the reliefs at Persepolis. Other Persian elements are the horses' close-cropped manes and their tails tied with a knot in the middle. But there is no trace of the bridle and harness reproduced in such detail in Persian portrayals of horses. The woman in the banquet scene wears a headdress that was properly the privilege of the Persian kings. But it is also worn by a high-born lady depicted on a cylinder seal with the seated figure of Anaitis. The lady on a cylinder seal in the British Museum wears a similar crown. The three servants, like those on the attic of the Sarcophagus with the Weeping Women, wear long chitons; this may well be a Persian or rather a Phoenician custom because at that time the Greeks wore only short tunics. The low boots worn by the cup-bearer and the servants on the other two stelae I have already mentioned more than once occur too on the reliefs at Persepolis. The style of Elnaf's beard and his prominent nose are also non-Greek. The woman, the cup-bearer and the servants also seem to have the same ethnical type. They may be Semites.

The hair style of the male figures, particularly Elnaf and the cup-bearer, conforms to the severe style of the early classical period that remained in vogue for a long time in Asia Minor. The blousy kolpos of the chiton occurs, it is true, on Persian reliefs but it had also been very popular with the East Greeks since archaic times.

The banquet scene, as represented here, though based on Assyrian models, has been greatly modified in the Greek sense. The oldest examples of such scenes in East Greek art are found on the terracotta reliefs from Larisa that date back to the second half of the sixth century. The tripod with the krater behind the cup-bearer on our stela already occurs in a banquet scene on one of those terracotta plaques. But the scene on the stela from Dascylium is linked with a group of East Greek banquet scenes in which the wife is seated and not reclining like the husband. Scenes of the same type can be observed on a Thasian relief, on the Satrap's Sarcophagus and on the relief from Çavusköy, all of which are preserved in the Istanbul Museum.

But our relief displays its Greek character in the artistic handling. The free movements of the figures and their lifelike gestures are couched in Greek idiom. The cup-bearer's stance tells us that the humble stone-cutter was aware of the classical manner of depicting a standing figure with the weight of the body resting on one leg, balancing the other with its bended knee, but lacked the skill to reproduce it perfectly. Technical details like the bulging eyes are also Greek. They are a characteristic feature of Ionian sculpture. The shape of the stela and of the palmette acroterium, which is no longer extant, as well as the moldings at top and bottom, are further specifically Greek elements. This stela is the work of an East Greek stone-cutter from Cyzicus or Dascylium who did his best to produce a relief in the Persian manner as commissioned by his customer. He conformed in some details to the caravan leader's tastes and wishes, but we can see from the style of his work that actually he was Greek.

The stela is remarkable for its slenderness. Assuming that it had the same proportions as the one on which the palmettes are still preserved, the acroterium accounted for a quarter of the total height. So the whole stela must have been one third taller than it is now. This exaggerated slenderness is characteristic of archaic Greek grave stelae. But the molding at the top is of a type that occurs in stelae of the fifth and fourth centuries. And the cup-bearer's stance, of which I have already spoken, tells us that this one cannot have been made before the end of the fifth century at the earliest.

Anatolia was not in a position to play a leading role while under Persian domination in the fifth century B.C. But we can see that works of outstanding quality were produced in Lycia towards the end of the fifth century and at the beginning of the fourth. The *Heroon* from Gölbaşi and still more the Nereid Monument at Xanthos count among the major achievements of the classical age. They are, it is true, strongly influenced by the art of Phidias but owe their power to their native Anatolian traits. The relief of the phalanx hastening into battle, once part of the Nereid Monument and now preserved in the British Museum, is an expressive work of the utmost significance. The impressive rhythmic effect achieved by the rows of identical figures is unparalleled in the art of the ancient world and the first really successful attempt at expressionistic composition in relief sculpture.

The appearance at Xanthos of a work of art of the class of the Nereid Monument warrants the belief that the sarcophagus from the royal necropolis at Sidon is also an authentic Lycian work. Not only has it the ogival lid of a Lycian sarcophagus hewn out of a cliff, but other Lycian motifs as well. For instance, the two lion-shaped lugs for raising the lid are typically Lycian. The subject matter of the reliefs displays links with other Lycian monuments. The sphinxes on the gable had been a popular motif in Lycia since preclassical times; they occur on the Payawa sarcophagus too. The four-horse chariots recall a sarcophagus from Merehi, on which there is a chimaera that brings to mind the crouching lions on the work we are discussing.

The reliefs on the sides represent men on horseback hunting a wild boar and Amazons on chariots hunting a lion; on the ends, centaurs in single combat; on the gables, griffins and the sphinxes I have already mentioned. The mounted men in the boar-hunt scene are considerably influenced by the cavalcade on the Parthenon frieze. The artist has endeavored to achieve the same effect without employing exactly the same iconographic types. But his figures lack the tension of the facial and bodily forms as well as the graceful, natural movements and postures we so greatly admire on the Parthenon reliefs. The poses of the two riders to left and right are lifeless and humdrum. Only the finely modelled features of the bearded horsemen express a certain passion and excitement that we miss in the other figures.

In the Amazons' heads one also looks in vain for the ethos of Phidian art; they have the sort of rigidity people sometimes have when deep in thought but not when engaged in violent action. Their broad faces and stocky bodies reveal the Peloponnesian origin of the sculptor, who has combined in this work the tradition of Lycia and Asia Minor with the Attic style and Peloponnesian spirit and taste. But he is somewhat wanting in artistic sensibility. For all that he is an excellent sculptor and his work displays the very highest sculptural quality. Worthy of note is the effect of depth given by his composition in the flat. This truly unparalleled achievement is the result of a masterly arrangement of the human and equine figures. The entire relief has a painterly character that is enhanced by the delicate handling of the plastic forms. This sarcophagus is a work in the Post-Parthenonic style and as such dates from about the beginning of the fourth century B.C.

In that same century the part played by Ionian art and Anatolian culture in the Hellenic world, though not of the first rank, was still very important. The buildings designed by the eminent Greek architect Pytheos, the Temple of Athena at Priene, paragon of the Ionic order, and the Mausoleum of Halicarnassus, one of the seven wonders of the world, are the greatest architectural works of their day. Other handsome, grandiose buildings were erected during that same period in several cities in western Asia Minor. Labranda, excavated by Swedish archaeologists, still possesses very well preserved ruins that give us a good idea of the architecture of that time. Worthy of

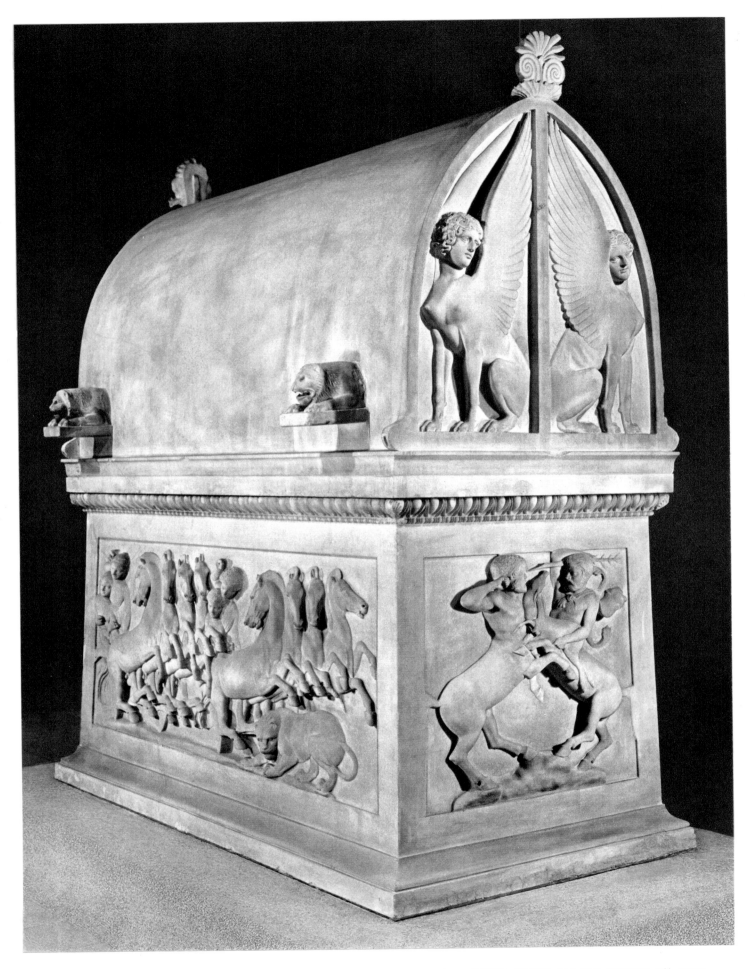

LYCIAN SARCOPHAGUS FROM THE ROYAL NECROPOLIS AT SIDON. PARIAN MARBLE. ABOUT 400 B.C. HEIGHT 9½ FEET.
ARCHAEOLOGICAL MUSEUM, ISTANBUL.

special mention are Louis Robert's excavations at Amyzon and Claros, which have contributed much to our knowledge of the Doric order in Asia Minor. The temple at Claros housed the most important oracle in Anatolia after the sanctuary at Didyma. Our thanks are due to Kristian Jeppesen, Roland Martin and Alfred Westholm for fundamental studies on the architecture of that age.

The Sarcophagus with the Weeping Women from the royal necropolis at Sidon is an excellent work from an East Greek workshop that flourished in one of the major centers of western Asia Minor during the fourth century. Like the Nereid Monument from Xanthos and the Mausoleum of Halicarnassus, it is shaped like an Ionic gable-roofed edifice, but lacks the high podium on which those two structures rest. Round its low, molded podium runs a Lesbian cyma surmounted by a frieze with many-figured hunting scenes. The half-columns rest on Attic-Ionic bases. The entablature is embellished with denticles as in the buildings of the same period designed by Pytheos, the Mausoleum and the Temple of Athena at Priene. The attic has a frieze like that on the cornice of the Artemision at Ephesus. Eighteen weeping female figures in long chiton and mantle stand before or lean against the parapet that links the half-columns. Other weeping women are depicted on the gable ends, while the attic is adorned with male mourners and funeral processions.

All these decorative elements refer to the life of the Phoenician prince entombed in the sarcophagus. He has been identified on historical and stylistic grounds with King Straton I, who died about 360 B.C. Tradition has it that he led a life of debauchery surrounded by courtesans imported from the Peloponnese. The eighteen women depicted on the sarcophagus presumably represent those courtesans mourning their lord and master.

The Sarcophagus with the Weeping Women is a carefully thought out work of a very high order. The sculptures are pure Greek in form and content. The frieze on the attic alone reveals foreign iconographic details. The vehicles are based on Persian models and the servants wear long robes that may be viewed as a Persian fashion. All in all it is a magnificent work of quite extraordinary significance. But, however well executed, the sculptural ornamentation comes off less well than the reliefs on the Mausoleum of Halicarnassus or on Attic tombstones. The mourners are portrayed in the lavish drapery of the fourth century. They display a close affinity with female figures on Attic tomb reliefs which can be ascribed, on the basis of stylistic connections, to the middle of that century. Hence the Sarcophagus with the Weeping Women should date from about 350 B.C.

The so-called Alexander Sarcophagus is not only one of the most famous of all archaeological finds but also one of the most important artistic achievements of the ancient world that have come down to us. It is the best preserved masterpiece of Greek art and its splendid colors still amaze those who contemplate it today. It came from the royal necropolis at Sidon, which was discovered and excavated by the great Turkish archaeologist Osman Hamdi, known to archaeological literature as Hamdi Bey. He took care that all important finds were taken to the Istanbul Museum and suffered no damage in transit.

The Alexander Sarcophagus is embellished with ornamental elements of the Ionic order executed with such superlative workmanship that they give the structure a superb appearance. The lid is shaped like a temple pediment with Ionic entablature and combines with the rim of the casket to form the crowning member of the sarcophagus. This is balanced by the equally tectonic podium, which is an essential element of Ionian architecture.

The relief on the front represents a battle in which Alexander the Great himself takes part. On the left we see him astride a rearing steed, hurling his spear at a Persian whose mount has fallen to its knees but who still endeavors to defend himself with the weapon he grips in his raised right hand. We can recognize Alexander by the lion's head—the attribute of Hercules—he wears. The group recalls the scene of Alexander's battle with the Persians on the famous mosaic from the House of the Faun at Pompeii now kept in the Naples Museum. In particular the posture of the Persian and his fallen horse leads us to infer that the sculptor of the sarcophagus was familiar with the painting by Philoxenos of Eretria from which the mosaic was copied.

To the right of this group are a Persian and a Greek in single combat and then a Persian aiming an arrow at Alexander. In the next group a mounted Greek brandishes his weapon to strike down a Persian who is begging for mercy. An almost naked Greek stops the horse of a galloping Persian, while in the foreground a Persian lets fly at a Greek who is charging at him; this last figure at the right-hand edge of the relief balances in free symmetry that of Alexander on the left. In between there is another scene in which a wounded Persian is caught by a comrade as he slips off his horse. On the ground lie the corpses of four Persians and a naked Greek.

The relief on the rear depicts a lion hunt in which men in both Persian and Greek costume are taking part. In the center is a rider whose costume and facial type show that he is a Persian. His mount has been attacked by a lion whose claws are tearing his chest. Five men, two on horseback and three on foot, are rushing to the rescue of the menaced Persian. One of those on foot is already striking at the lion with an axe, while a hound is biting its hindleg. The two mounted men, one from the right, the other from the left, are jabbing at the beast with their lances. The Persian at the left-hand edge of the relief is shooting an arrow at the lion: gripping the bow with the left hand, he is drawing the string with the right. In front of him a naked Greek rushes in to help, his cloak slung over his left arm. Two hounds are also running in from the left to attack the lion. At the right-hand edge of the relief there is a scene that has no connection with the lion hunt. Here a Greek and a Persian are busy dispatching a stag. The Greek holds the beast by the antlers and is about to stab it with a spear; the Persian is swinging an axe to deliver the death blow.

The horseman in the center of the lion hunt has been identified, perhaps correctly, with the Phoenician king Abdalonymos. He is dressed like a Persian, "in the costume of the noble caste of which he was proud to count himself a member." After the Battle of Issus (333 B.C.) Abdalonymos was set on his father's throne by Hephaistion at Alexander's bidding. There is a story that he once sent a fine perfume to Alexander. It is therefore quite natural that he had his sarcophagus decorated with scenes from the life of his patron and liege.

SARCOPHAGUS OF THE WEEPING WOMEN FROM THE ROYAL NECROPOLIS AT SIDON. PENTELIC MARBLE. ABOUT 350 B.C. HEIGHT 71″.
ARCHAEOLOGICAL MUSEUM, ISTANBUL.

We may see a second representation of Alexander in the rider behind Abdalonymos, in the lion-hunt scene. He differs from the other Greeks on these reliefs by wearing a fillet round his head. His lance is balanced in his hanging right hand just as in the Alexander Mosaic from the House of the Faun at Pompeii, which I have already mentioned. It is quite unimportant that this image bears no great resemblance to the extant portraits of Alexander. Indeed, the image in the battle scene is no better a likeness: so much so that, were it not for the lion's head, we should have hesitated to identify him. The sculptor seems to have idealized Alexander's features intentionally. On the whole, in fact, he has given his naked, heroicized figures generic, idealized faces. As Furtwängler rightly says, his aim was not to depict individual figures and historical events. He conformed to one of the basic canons of Greek art of the classical period —namely, that the artist should raise what was individual and temporal to a lofty, ideal plane and only render timeless, typical beauty. There is another alternative:

THE ALEXANDER SARCOPHAGUS FROM THE ROYAL NECROPOLIS AT SIDON. PENTELIC MARBLE. LATE 4TH CENTURY B.C. HEIGHT 77″.
ARCHAEOLOGICAL MUSEUM, ISTANBUL.

THE ALEXANDER SARCOPHAGUS FROM THE ROYAL NECROPOLIS AT SIDON, DETAIL: GREEKS AND PERSIANS FIGHTING.
PENTELIC MARBLE. LATE 4TH CENTURY B.C. ARCHAEOLOGICAL MUSEUM, ISTANBUL.

the sculptor and his client may have been tactful enough to be satisfied with allusions and consider it unbecoming to exploit the likeness of the conqueror of the world to enhance their own personal fame.

The narrow ends of the sarcophagus repeat in simpler version the themes treated on the long sides. On one we see Persians and Greeks fighting. A Persian on a rearing horse occupies the center; he is trying to stab with his lance a fallen Greek who is protecting himself very successfully with his shield. To right and left are Greeks and Persians fighting in pairs. The other end represents a hunting scene in which only Persians are taking part.

The Alexander Sarcophagus is pure Greek both in form and content. There are no eastern elements relating to the sculptor's employer. The griffins above the cornice are of the same type as the Persian lion-griffins but have long been known in Asia Minor; similar ones occur on the tomb from Belevi near Ephesus erected about the middle of the fourth century. Alexander and two other Macedonians wear short tunics with long sleeves. This might refer to the fact that in Persia he adopted local dress. The Persians are clad in long, skin-tight, gaily colored trews, a colored tunic with long, tight-fitting sleeves and an overgarment also with sleeves but worn like a cape. It is the *kandys*, whose wearer let it hang free from the shoulders, only putting his arms through the sleeves when parading before the king. The head-dress of the figures clothed in Persian costume is a limp tiara that covers the lower part of the face as far as the under-lip.

The sarcophagus is made of Pentelic, i.e. Attic, marble. The reliefs display many traits and motifs typical not only of Attica but also of other regions of mainland Greece and already long known in Asia Minor. Observing these reliefs one cannot help thinking of the frieze of the Mausoleum of Halicarnassus. The two pairs of fighters on one of the narrow ends of the Alexander Sarcophagus recall certain panels of the frieze, namely those attributed to Scopas.

But it seems to me that for very simple reasons there is very little hope of identifying the sculptor of the Sarcophagus. His cannot possibly have been a name to conjure with, because famous artists who worked exclusively in bronze and produced images of the gods could hardly have been interested in executing for a minor king in a barbarous land a colossal but merely decorative monument that was destined to disappear underground as soon as it was finished. So a less known artist accepted the job though it could not enhance his reputation. Yet he produced a work that is an outstanding exemplar of his day. Though no pioneer, he was an excellent sculptor and a first-rate adept of a rather out-dated artistic style that had been fashionable at the middle of the century. His figures are well proportioned, their postures and movements graceful and balanced. The composition is based on a free symmetry that is most effective. His animals too, at least the horses, are magnificent achievements. The impact of the

STATUE OF ALEXANDER THE GREAT BY MENAS OF PERGAMUM. MARBLE. FROM MAGNESIA AD SIPYLUM,
SECOND HALF OF THE SECOND CENTURY B.C. HEIGHT 75″. ARCHAEOLOGICAL MUSEUM, ISTANBUL.

GREAT FRIEZE OF THE ALTAR OF PERGAMUM, DETAIL: NYX, GODDESS OF NIGHT, HURLING A VASE AT A FALLEN GIANT.
MARBLE. ABOUT 180 B.C. HEIGHT 90″. PERGAMONMUSEUM, BERLIN.

lifelike figures is heightened by the color, which has been almost entirely preserved. Violet, purple, red, maroon, yellow and blue are employed in a wide range. Pale colors and half tones predominate. Paint is applied to hair, eyes, lashes, brows and lips, as well as to entire costumes. The flesh is not painted over but merely tinted with a light wash.

The artist's strong point is the extremely lifelike rendering of heads and faces, whose passionate expressions are most engaging. Particularly effective is the application to the eyes of painted highlights. The shining eyes give some of the heads a fascinating beauty. This splendid, indeed unique work was probably executed after 330 B.C. but may have been done during Alexander's lifetime.

The cities of Asia Minor vied with Alexandria and Rhodes as the leading centers of art and culture during the Hellenistic period, namely the last three centuries before Christ, which was so important for the history of the world. The most ancient Corinthian temple is still preserved in Asia Minor; its considerable ruins are located at Olba to the north of Silifke. Two other very important edifices of the same period that deserve to be mentioned here are the Council Hall at Miletus, whose ground-plan is well preserved, and the Theater at Priene, which has come down to us in very good condition. Hermogenes, one of the greatest of Greek architects, to whom Ionian architecture owes

Pergamum, or Pergamon, is one of the most significant of the ancient ruined cities of Anatolia. Excavations of the site began as long ago as 1878, under German archaeologists, and the finds made between then and 1886 were almost as sensational as Schliemann's discoveries at Troy. The work of excavation was later resumed and has been carried on intermittently by three generations of archaeologists, bringing to light fine buildings and sculptures of the third and second centuries B.C., which in many cases were later restored by the Romans.

The most important building was the temple of Athena, which must have been erected in the time of Eumenes I (263-241 B.C.). It was a Doric peripteral temple of two storeys, with six columns in front and ten on each side; its porticoes and gate-house were built by Eumenes II (197-159 B.C.). The north and east porticoes had Doric columns on the lower storey, Ionic columns on the upper. The upper colonnade was closed by a balustrade carrying a battle frieze. The columns and entablature of the temple, together with the reconstructed entrance hall, are preserved in the Pergamon Museum in Berlin. A piece of statuary, "The Gaul and his Wife", stood in the court of the temple. On the north side of it was the Pergamene library containing 200,000 volumes. In front of the library stood the colossal statue of Athena Parthenos, a Hellenistic version of the famous work by Phidias; it too is now in the Pergamon Museum, Berlin.

Other buildings of the Hellenistic period are the temples of Hera and Demeter and the Great Altar of Zeus (described in the text). The gigantic gymnasium built on three levels on the lower acropolis and the impressive theater on the upper acropolis were erected by the Pergamene kings, but extensively rebuilt in Roman imperial times. The temple of Trajan, north of the library, and the Ionic temple north of the theater terrace both date to the Roman period. Eumenes II surrounded the city with a fine defensive wall, considerable parts of which can still be seen. In the second century A.D. Pergamum numbered 120,000 inhabitants.

a number of enrichments and progressive innovations, lived and worked in Asia Minor during the second century. The ground-plans of the temples he built at Magnesia on the Maeander and at Teos are still well preserved.

The first artistic center in Asia Minor during the Hellenistic age was Pergamum. Its heyday was the reign of Eumenes II, whose great altar to Zeus and Athena on the citadel was erected about 180 B.C. The reliefs from that grandiose monument, now preserved in Berlin, are the best examples of Hellenistic sculpture. They ostensibly represent the war between the gods and the giants, but refer by transposition to the victory of Pergamum over the Gauls. Their style has a baroque quality that may be viewed as an exaggeration of the general artistic trend in the fourth century. The hair is loose and cut in deep lines that produce violent effects of light and shade. More typical still are the pathetic, upward-gazing eyes, deep-set in strongly arched orbits under crooked, bushy brows, and the parted lips. The faces express with the utmost clarity passionate excitement, pain or anger. The muscles bulge excessively, the drapery is marked by tumbled diagonal folds that form deep shadows. The bodily movements are impetuous and stormy. Novel statuary types were invented, whose impact was felt later. For instance, Erika Simon has recently pointed out Pergamonic influences in the frescoes in the Villa of the Mysteries near Pompeii.

But not all the male faces have such extravagantly pained expressions: there are also some handsome heads set on splendidly proportioned bodies. The female figures as a rule are charming. The most beautiful and best preserved are those of Artemis and Nyx. The latter (reproduced here) is the goddess of night. In her right hand she holds a vase with a snake coiled round it, which she is about to hurl at a giant. She is tall and slender with beautiful neck and charming head. Her face has an almost childlike expression of graceful excitement. Another engaging figure on the same frieze is Aphrodite, whose beautiful head was recently discovered in the Istanbul Museum by Heinz Luschey.

The statue of Alexander the Great from Magnesia on Mount Sipylos, now in the Istanbul Museum, is also a work of the school of Pergamum. An inscription found on the same site as the statue runs as follows: "Menas of Pergamum, son of Aias, made (it)." Alexander stands facing the beholder. His right leg bears the weight of his body; his bent left knee is turned slightly outwards. The right arm, no longer extant, rested on a spear. The left arm hangs slack, the hand gripping a sword, of which only a fragment of the hilt can still be distinguished. In a portrait of Alexander on a gem in Leningrad the left hand holds the sword in the same way. And in a statuette from Priene, now in Berlin, Alexander also held a sword with his left hand, as we can see from the fragment that has been preserved. A number of holes drilled in the head show that the full head of hair was formerly crowned with a metal wreath—presumably laurel because here Alexander appears to be portrayed in the guise of Apollo. That is confirmed by certain details of the head which is rather carefully rendered. As we can see from the herma

COLOSSAL HEAD OF ANTIOCHOS I OF COMMAGENE. NIMRUD DAĞ, WEST TERRACE. FIRST HALF OF THE FIRST CENTURY B.C.

in Paris, which derives from Lysippus, Alexander's hair grew in a peculiar and very personal manner. It stood up in front like a lion's mane and fell symmetrically at the sides. This also occurs on the fine head from Pergamum in the Istanbul Museum.

Menas did not insist on this characteristic trait and, since his aim was to portray Alexander in the guise of Apollo, decided that the sword was sufficient to identify his model. The smooth, calm forms of the face and the moderate pathos of the eyes also befit the divine nature of the god. The only clothing is a mantle that covers the body from the hips down, as well as part of the left shoulder and arm, but leaves the trunk bare.

This work resembles the statue of Zeus found in the Temple of Hera at Pergamum erected under Attalos II (159-138 B.C.). The postures of the body, legs and left hand are similar and so is the arrangement of the mantle. The statue of Poseidon from Melos, now in the National Museum at Athens, is of the same type. The god leans on a spear, as Menas' Alexander presumably did. The latter, though the arrangement of the drapery is quite different, probably dates from the middle or second half of the second century, like the Zeus from Pergamum.

Magnificent sculptures of colossal dimensions dating from the late Hellenistic period have been preserved on the 7000-foot Nimrud Dağ in southwest Anatolia; they were erected by Antiochos I of Commagene during the first half of the first century B.C. On the summit of the mountain the sovereign himself was portrayed in a statue almost 30 feet tall surrounded by the local gods before a tumulus over 160 feet high. These works, which combine elegance with beauty, represent a tempered, idealized version of the Hellenistic style. They are pure Greek in form, but as regards subject matter and iconography keep to the native Anatolian tradition. The excavations in Commagene carried out by Theresa Goell and Friedrich Karl Dörner have given uncommonly important results.

In Roman times the Greco-Anatolian tradition continued almost without a break, so that Roman art in Asia Minor presents a certain originality. The statue of a boy from Tralles, now in the Istanbul Museum, dates from the early Empire period in Anatolia. For excellence of execution and artistic conception it can hold its own against the deservedly famous masterpieces of the foregoing Greek period. It represents an adolescent athlete who has just finished his daily workout or perhaps won a victory in an important contest. After a cold bath in the open air within the precincts of the gymnasium he has donned his tunic and wrapped himself in his cloak. He is completely exhausted, so before going home he rests a while against the post that marks the start or finish of the race course. To become the public's undisputed darling has cost him years of tireless training in athletics and particularly wrestling. His thick ears prove that he has fought hard since childhood. In fact, one of the holds practised

STATUE OF A YOUNG ATHLETE (DETAIL) FROM TRALLES (AYDIN). PARIAN MARBLE. REIGN OF AUGUSTUS (27 B.C.-14 A.D.). ARCHAEOLOGICAL MUSEUM, ISTANBUL.

STATUE OF A YOUNG ATHLETE FROM TRALLES (AYDIN). PARIAN MARBLE. REIGN OF AUGUSTUS
(27 B.C.-14 A.D.). HEIGHT 58″. ARCHAEOLOGICAL MUSEUM, ISTANBUL.

by the Greek fighters of old, and indeed by Turkish wrestlers today, consists in catching an opponent by the head and pressing the ears so hard against the skull that they became permanently thickened.

The artist had a good idea to use the stadium finishing post as a prop for his statue —perhaps the very post that the boy had touched first in the race. It provides a very fitting natural background. The weight of the body does not rest on the right leg alone but is also partly supported by the post; in this way the leaning posture gives a vivid impression of fatigue. The left leg is crossed over the right and presumably only the tip of the left foot rested on the ground. The cavity at the lower end of the right leg proves that the missing feet were carved in a separate block of marble and attached later. Charming effects are achieved with the arrangement of the drapery. The contours of the body disappear entirely under the finely modelled folds of the thick material. The boy's left arm rests on his chest; his right arm hangs slack by his side. Their vague outlines are just barely visible. The plain folds form a pleasant contrast with the delicate handling of the heavy cloth. The manner in which the body is concealed reminds one slightly of the statue of Aspasia, which is a copy dating from the age of Augustus. In modelling this drapery the Tralles artist may have been inspired by some contemporary work copied, like the Aspasia, from early classical models. In other respects, however, he was chiefly influenced by Polycletus. The pose of the head is reminiscent of the so-called Westmacott Youth in the British Museum, while the handling of the hair brings to mind Augustan copies of the Doryphoros. The hair-style itself, with the parting above the forehead, is unmistakably Augustan.

The comparisons I have made prove that the Young Athlete from Tralles is a classicistic original dating from the Augustan period. Classicism was the prevalent style at the time our artist lived and worked. Like all his contemporaries, he had to adjust to the general taste of the day. What is important is that he succeeded in giving the boy's face a delicate, childlike expression. He has lent him the noble features and fine, large eyes characteristic of the Mediterranean races. This work has an unusual charm that cannot fail to affect men's hearts and souls through the centuries.

THE ROMAN PERIOD IN ANATOLIA

In the first and second centuries of our era the Anatolian cities were the richest and most important centers of art and culture. We know them from the very extensive ruins that still exist in large numbers and excellent state of preservation. Some have already been excavated; others are being systematically explored at the present time. At Pergamum digging continues with good results under Erich Boehringer. The excavation of Ephesus, carried out after the First World War by Joseph Keil and after the Second by Franz Miltner, is now in the hands of Fritz Eichler and yields new, highly significant finds every year. At Hierapolis Italian archaeologists under Paolo Verzone have done some first-class work. At Aphrodisias Kenan Erim has been digging for several years on behalf of New York University; he has already discovered some very important buildings and brought to light a large number of works of outstanding quality by the famous local school of sculpture. Side and Perga, both of which are situated in Pamphylia on the middle stretch of the south coast of Anatolia, have for the last two years been thoroughly and systematically explored by the Turkish archaeologist Arif Müfid Mansel. His splendid finds are housed in a handsome museum erected at Side.

Of all this rich Roman period in Anatolia I must rest content with describing only one sculpture and two buildings. First the colossal statue of Artemis of Ephesus. Executed in the reign of Domitian (81-96 A.D.), it was brought to light, with many other important works of art, by Franz Miltner who injected new energy into the excavation of Ephesus. Miltner, whose premature death was a great misfortune, has given us a masterly description of the statue. Here are his own words.

"If I am not quite mistaken, about the same time as Domitian's temple was built, the portico-framed space in front of the sanctuary of Hestia in the Prytaneion was embellished by the erection in its center of a statue of the Artemis of Ephesus about twice life size on a simple pedestal. Including the tall head-dress it must have towered about 16 feet on its base. The mighty image of the great goddess dominated the square and the impression of overwhelming power it gave must have been enhanced by the contrast between the compact mass of the figure and the delicate Ionic columns of the portico. Neither stylistic evolution nor the artist's taste could alter the shape of the divine image. It rose almost like a pillar, with legs pressed together, elbows sharply bent, arms outstretched and the palms of the hands turned upwards to indicate the goddess's eternal liberality. At her side stood the slender figures of the two hinds that always accompanied the deity, who was the protectress and defender of the whole animal kingdom. Other tokens of her power over wild beasts were the many symbols blazoned in high relief on her costume: the foreparts of bulls, griffins, sphinxes,

STATUE OF ARTEMIS (DIANA) OF EPHESUS. MARBLE. REIGN OF DOMITIAN (81-96 A.D.).
EPHESUS MUSEUM.

THE ROMAN STADIUM AT APHRODISIAS. SECOND CENTURY A.D.

chimaeras and lions, arranged one above the other in groups of three. They were meant
to denote all the forces over which the goddess held absolute sway since the dawn of
time. From the waist down the lateral panels of her dress are adorned with representations of bees; for the insect, thus closely linked with the deity, had from time imme-
morial been the city's heraldic emblem and occurs again and again on its coins. The
upper part of the body deserves special attention. The high neckline of the undergar-
ment is adorned with figures of Nike brandishing the thyrsos and apparently dancing
on the heavy, many-stranded rope of pearls that edges the bodice, which looks like
a physical deformity. Various signs of the zodiac are embroidered on the plain surface
directly below the pearls; still further down comes an ornament consisting of numerous egg-shaped objects. Some scholars unaware of the real significance of this feature
took them for multiple female breasts. That was how the Artemis of Ephesus came

to be called 'the many-breasted,' and attempts were made to find an explanation of this abnormality that might prove at least half-way credible. But the idea of the indiscriminate multiplication of a female sexual organ has never occurred to any nation; on purely aesthetic grounds it is unthinkable for the Greeks and quite out of keeping with the ancient Anatolians' primordial belief—in some ways hardly comprehensible at that depth—in the supreme authority of the Eternal Mother. A closer examination of the statue makes it clear that the artist always thought of the deity as having two breasts and viewed the curious multiple structure as part of her costume. Moreover, the study of customs and their formal expressions that have so often become incomprehensible proves beyond question the importance of the egg as symbol of eternal fecundity. The goddess's ornament is undoubtedly made of eggs or eggshells as a token that, though she was a virgin, her life-giving fecundity was inexhaustible. The images of fabulous beasts we have seen on her robe are repeated on the head-dress, which ends in a row of temple-like structures.

"The artist made a not unsuccessful attempt to master the delicate female forms at the back of the statue where the austerity of the divine image allowed him greater latitude than elsewhere, and the goddess stands on the square, not lovely but regal, and appears to the beholder as an unapproachable sovereign who is only moved by her gracious benevolence to give of her overflowing abundance. She is the divine protectress and defender who guards the entrance to the surrounding portico and to the chamber where the city's hearth is eternally alight. We only have to take one look at this statue to understand how the people could stand for hours in the theater shouting: 'Great is Artemis of the Ephesians!'"

The stadium at Aphrodisias and the theater at Aspendos are two grandiose edifices erected in Anatolia during the Roman period. The first is the best preserved example of an antique stadium to be found anywhere. The two still extant at Priene and Perga are in good condition, but the one at Aphrodisias is intact and gives an excellent idea of what a sports ground looked like in the ancient world. The stadium measures 885 feet long by 177 feet broad and with its fine proportions makes an uncommonly pleasant and impressive effect.

The theater at Aspendos is the best preserved theatrical building of antiquity, besides being one of the finest ancient buildings still extant in Anatolia. It is a magnificent example of an ancient theater designed in the Roman style of architecture and indeed the climax of a development that commenced at the end of the classical age. The architecture of the Hellenistic period made some essential advances in theater design, as we can see in the theater at Priene. But perfect unity of composition as we find it exemplified at Aspendos was only attained by the Romans. A Greek theater as a rule represents a harmonious fusion of architecture with the surrounding countryside. At Epidaurus, for example, the spectators sat in the midst of a landscape that was visible from every seat. A Roman theater, on the contrary, as Willy Zschietzschmann has so aptly observed, cuts itself off from the outer world and endeavors to compose all its parts in a self-contained space.

The theater at Aspendos gives the impression of a Greek theater leaning against the slope of a hill, yet is actually built entirely of stone. The architect was anxious to conform to the age-old tradition of a theater erected on the side of a hill. The auditorium, which in Roman times was usually semicircular, here is horseshoe-shaped.

THE ROMAN THEATER AT ASPENDOS: VIEW OF THE INTERIOR. SECOND HALF OF THE SECOND CENTURY A.D.

THE ROMAN THEATER AT ASPENDOS: THE BACK WALL OF THE STAGE (SCAENAE FRONS). SECOND HALF OF THE SECOND CENTURY A.D.

Impressive ruins of a number of important Roman cities lie along the southern coast of Asia Minor. Among the most interesting of them are Side, Perga and Aspendos. Side has a fine, well-preserved theater overlooking the sea. The defensive wall of breccia masonry built around the city in late Hellenistic times is still well preserved in places. The area around the main gate of the fortifications was converted in Roman imperial times, towards the end of the second century A.D., into a splendid courtyard, whose remains are still very attractive. Equally impressive are the remains of the nymphaeum, built under the Antonines, and of a magnificent façade with rich architectural and sculptural adornments. Of the two Roman temples by the sea, dating to the second century A.D., only the ground-plan can now be traced.

Perga is one of the best preserved of the ancient cities of Asia Minor. Very considerable remains of the theater and the stadium, both dating to the period of the Roman Empire, can still be seen. Particularly fine and impressive is the main gate of the fortifications, measuring over forty-five feet in height.

Aspendos was also an important city in this part of Asia Minor (ancient Pamphylia), and many of its buildings have come down to us in a remarkably good state of preservation, notably the market halls, the basilica, the nymphaeum and a splendid aqueduct. The finest of all, however, and the best preserved, is the Roman theater.

This effect may be due to architectural considerations: in fact, a perfectly semi-circular auditorium would not give the theater such a handsomely proportioned apse-shaped rear as it has now. In other respects the building at Aspendos displays all the features of Roman theaters. The side entrances, which in Greek theaters are always slanting, here are perpendicular and, what is more, arched over. The auditorium is bisected horizontally by a wide gallery. The lower part has nine tiers of seats with ten stairways; the upper part has twenty tiers with twenty-one stairways. As in all Roman theaters, the auditorium is topped by a pillared arcade with groined vaulting.

The back wall of the stage *(scaenae frons)*, which is two storeys high and once had a timber roof, rises above a low platform *(proskenion)* on which the play was acted. The *scaenae frons* had five doors that gave entry to the *proskenion*. The large one in the middle was called Porta Regia, the four smaller ones Portae Hospitales. The whole wall was embellished with a plethora of columns and other architectural features, from whose ruins we can largely appreciate the original symmetrical design.

The outside of the building exactly matches the internal arrangement. A row of arches on the rear outer wall responds to the arcade that crowns the auditorium, and the two-storey articulation of the stage is reproduced on the façade. A buttress and the tower-like portal were added later in the Seljuk period. Otherwise the façade of the Roman edifice has been preserved unchanged. A simple molding marks the dividing line between the two storeys; the row of seventeen upper windows is on a level with the arcade atop the auditorium. But when decorating the façade the architect relied more on the effect of simple architectural forms and so gave his work an impressive outline. The inscriptions still extant prove that the building was erected in the middle or second half of the second century A.D.

BYZANTIUM

CHRIST FROM THE DEESIS MOSAIC, LATE THIRTEENTH CENTURY. GALLERY OF ST SOPHIA, ISTANBUL.

WE know Byzantine art only by its fragments, as Charles Diehl has rightly remarked. Today these fragments are scattered far and wide. The lands over which, at one time or another, the Byzantine Empire held sway extend from the foothills of the Caucasus to the straits of Gibraltar; and if we add to this the area of Byzantine radiation, we have to include Russia as far north as Novgorod. Most of these lands still contain some Byzantine remains that are, so to speak, irremovable: buildings, architectural sculpture, mural painting, mosaic floors. Objects that could be readily transported, however, and in particular those luxury products for which Byzantium was famous in the Middle Ages—gold and silver, ivory and enamel, silken stuffs and illuminated manuscripts—are even more widely dispersed. Commercial exchange and diplomatic gifts, the loot of the Crusades, the avid collecting of European princes during the Renaissance and the even more systematic rapacity of modern museums have drained Byzantine objects from the country of their origin.

This migration of art objects has affected particularly that area which formed the very core of the Byzantine Empire, namely what is now Turkey. After centuries of war and depredation the number of movable Byzantine artifacts on Turkish soil has shrunk to very little: not a single carved ivory, enamel or textile that is worth mentioning, only one illuminated manuscript of major interest, a handful of icons. What remains—apart from some recent finds—is what could not be moved away. Yet, how vastly important is this residue! It stands to reason that the most perfect examples of Byzantine architecture and decoration should have been concentrated in the capital, Constantinople, and in the most vital provincial area, Asia Minor. Until very recently, however, these monuments have been but imperfectly known. As a result, the history of Byzantine art and in particular of Byzantine mural painting has been written largely on the basis of peripheral monuments to the exclusion of the center. It is only in the last thirty years that the uncovering of the mosaics of St Sophia, of the Great Palace pavement, of Kahriye Camii and Fethiye Camii has revealed to us the true quality of

figurative art in Constantinople. It is not much longer since we have come to know the bizarre rock churches of Cappadocia which have opened up to us the substratum of Byzantine culture in Asia Minor. Much else remains to be discovered or even to be recorded. Indeed, one can confidently predict that future advances in our knowledge of Early Christian and Byzantine art will be, to a large extent, made on the territory of Turkey.

Byzantine history may be said to begin with the foundation of Constantinople (324-330). Today, the visitor to Istanbul will find few mementoes of Constantine's original city. The immense Hippodrome still remains as an open space, and on its longitudinal

CONSTANTINE'S PORPHYRY COLUMN AS SEEN TODAY IN ISTANBUL.

THE EMPEROR THEODOSIUS I RECEIVING THE HOMAGE OF BARBARIANS, A.D. 390.
PEDESTAL OF THE EGYPTIAN OBELISK IN THE HIPPODROME, ISTANBUL.

axis still stands the mutilated trunk of the Delphic Serpent made by the victorious Greeks after the battle of Plataea (479 B.C.). This is the only surviving relic of the hundreds of antique statues which Constantine caused to be removed from the principal cities of the Greek East in order to decorate his capital. Of Constantine's palace, which he built next to the Hippodrome on the site now occupied by the mosque of Sultan Ahmed, nothing remains. But the monument which marked the "navel" of the Constantinian city is still standing: it is the Porphyry Column called by the Turks Çemberlitaş (the Hooped Stone). Set up in 328, it stood in the middle of an elliptical forum bordered by the Senate House and other public buildings. A flight of five steps, now buried in the ground, leads up to a broad platform upon which is placed a pedestal of white marble. The shaft consists of seven drums of Egyptian porphyry, the juncture of the drums being concealed by wreaths of laurel leaves. The original capital was perhaps of the Corinthian order and it supported a gilded statue of Apollo-Helios identified with Constantine himself. Today, this column presents a sad spectacle: a drawing made in 1574 helps us, however, to grasp something of its original appearance. The statue and capital were thrown down by a storm in 1106 and replaced by a masonry topping; the pedestal and the lowest drum were enclosed in 1779 by a protective envelope of stonework; the shaft, cracked and blackened by fire, is held together by an iron armature. Even in this battered condition, the column gives us an idea of its spectacular costliness. Porphyry was the most precious stone known in antiquity; never before in the Roman world had such a mass of porphyry (each drum weighs 63 tons) been expended on a single monument.

In the first century of its existence Constantinople underwent a spectacular urban development. Constantine's city, considered too big when it was first laid out, was soon expanded to include seven hills. In every respect the New Rome had to be like the Old, only, if possible, bigger and flashier. There were, as in Rome, fourteen urban regions; the complex of palace and hippodrome was modelled after the Palatine; there was a Capitol and a Senate House or, to be more exact, there were two Senate Houses; the Milliarium Aureum, a simple column in Rome, was surpassed by the Milion of Constantinople, an elaborate arch decorated with statues. Rome had two historiated columns with spiral decoration, those of Trajan and Marcus Aurelius; Constantinople had to have two of its own, and these were set up by Theodosius I (379-395) and his son Arcadius (395-408) respectively. The column of Theodosius was demolished around 1500, but a few of the reliefs that decorated its shaft have survived. We know more about the column of Arcadius which lasted down to 1715, and the pedestal of which is still standing. A monotonous succession of battle scenes and triumphal processions spiralled, as usual, round its shaft. The column was about 164 feet high, taller therefore than the two in Rome, yet it commemorated nothing more glorious than the liquidation of a rebellious Gothic general who had been in the service of the Roman government. The same passion for size is exemplified by a Corinthian capital derived from an as yet unidentified monument that was recently dug up in the courtyard of the Seraglio. Over seven and a half feet high and nine feet wide, this is surely one of the biggest capitals in existence. The style of the carving and the presence of grotesque heads, one on each side (as also in the column of the Emperor Marcian), point to a date in the fifth century.

These few remains may serve to evoke, however partially, the mighty and somewhat tasteless pomp of the christianized Roman Empire. They also serve to illustrate one of the most significant facets of the nascent Byzantine art, what we may call its *étatisme*. To save the Roman world from disintegration, the Emperors Diocletian and Constantine invented one of the most crushing bureaucratic systems known to man. Every aspect of life was regulated and regimented. The working classes, both the servile *coloni* who cultivated the big estates and the skilled workers who were organized into hereditary corporations, were irretrievably tied to their callings. They supported the twin pyramids, carefully separated but similarly organized, of the civil and military hierarchies. This machinery was so constructed that it could be operated from one point only, the emperor's Sacred Palace. Raised beyond the ken of ordinary mortals, the emperor was the center of a palatine liturgy. His comings and goings, his vestments and comportment were meticulously and theatrically ordered so as to produce an almost supernatural impression. And what was enacted in the palace was reflected, in diminishing scale, at the courts of the various dignitaries each one of whom was surrounded by his own circle of clients.

This kind of system has a predictable effect on the arts: it produces rhetoric whether in words or in stone. Freedom and spontaneity are banished. That the literature of the later Empire is blanketed with rhetoric and adulation it is hardly necessary to prove. In the visual arts the result was the same. A good example is provided by the base of the Egyptian obelisk in the Hippodrome of Constantinople. This carved pedestal dates from 390 A.D., when the obelisk was raised by order of Theodosius I. On each of the four sides of the pedestal a similar scene is represented with slight variations: the emperor presiding over the games. Seated motionless with members of his family in his special loge, the emperor looks straight ahead; his bodyguard stand stiffly on either side, the senators below. Further down, a file of barbarian envoys crawl on their knees, bringing their gifts to the emperor in token of submission. In spite of its soft modelling, the scene has an air of stiff hieratic dignity. The offering of gifts was only one of several standard themes designed to glorify the emperor: there were, in addition, the emperor's triumphal arrival *(adventus)*, the emperor trampling on the necks of the vanquished *(calcatio)*, and others equally unpleasant.

The downward reflection of imperial imagery may be seen in another pedestal, discovered in 1962 and now in the Archaeological Museum of Istanbul. It supported a statue of the charioteer Porphyrios and dates from about 500 A.D. Porphyrios, an idol of the urban populace, is represented on all four sides as a *triumphator*, brandishing the

MARBLE PEDESTAL WHICH ORIGINALLY SUPPORTED A STATUE OF THE CHARIOTEER PORPHYRIOS, ABOUT A.D. 500.
ARCHAEOLOGICAL MUSEUM, ISTANBUL.

TOMBSTONE OF A.D. 285. KÜTAHYA MUSEUM.

crown of victory as he stands erect in his chariot. Behind him hovers a figure of the Fortuna of Constantinople, cornucopia in hand. At the corners of the pedestal winged victories act as caryatids. And below, pygmy-like, stand the acclaiming spectators of the hippodrome.

The monument of Porphyrios cannot be called a work of art, but the very debasement of its style is of interest. Setting aside the ineptitude of the workmanship, there is a troubling disharmony in the work which results from the use of a classical repertoire in a completely unclassical manner. The sense of depth which the subject requires is here lacking so that the Fortuna appears to be growing out of Porphyrios's head, and the diminutive spectators to be standing on a flat parapet rather than on the receding benches of a hippodrome. Equally troubling to our eyes is the disregard for scale: the discrepancy between the caryatids and Porphyrios, between Porphyrios and his tiny horses, between the figures in the upper register and those in the lower. Size has become here a factor of the figure's status, not of its position in space. The sculptor's propensity for flat decorative work conflicts with the lingering classicism of the subject-matter. Here we touch on a basic symptom of late Roman and early Byzantine art: to account for it we have to retrace our steps.

The classicism of Roman imperial art formed a thin surface crust. Already in the third century, when the fabric of the Empire was so severely shaken, this crust began to crack in all directions. Classicism pertained to the ruling aristocracy; it was not a natural form of expression for provinces that were imperfectly romanized or hellenized. In various parts of the Roman world, but especially in the east (Egypt, Syria, Asia Minor) we notice, even before the third century, the appearance of what has been aptly called "sub-antique" art. In the territory of Turkey this trend can be studied in hundreds of tombstones of the second and third centuries A.D. that were made for average provincials—farmers, traders, soldiers, etc. A specimen from the museum of Kütahya, dated A.D. 285, may serve as illustration. Within an arched frame decorated with a vine scroll, the deceased and two children stand stiffly at attention. Setting aside their classical costume and the attributes they hold, we would hardly have guessed that this was a monument of the Greco-Roman world. The style is governed by strict frontality and disregard for the third dimension. The heads and hands are too big for the bodies, and the eyes, staring fixedly ahead, are particularly prominent. The drapery has been reduced to a formal pattern, and the same may be said of the elaborately curled hair. We are reminded of the Palmyrene sculptures of the first and second centuries A.D.; in our relief, however, barbarization has been carried one step further.

When we stop to think that this work is roughly contemporary with the "Sidamara" sarcophagi that were also produced in Asia Minor, but for a different class of customers, we begin to understand the artistic dichotomy which Byzantine art inherited in the fourth century. The Kütahya gravestone illustrates the level to which the ordinary stonecarver naturally tended; the "Sidamara" sarcophagi, on the other hand, show us what the cultivated class considered proper. All the principal elements of medieval style are already before us: there is no need to look for exotic influences coming from Persia or Central Asia, as several prominent scholars would have us do.

Henceforth, the preponderance of one or the other style will depend on the cultural tone set by the imperial court and the degree of sophistication attained by the ruling classes. In the reign of Constantine primitivism appeared to be gaining the upper hand as we may judge, for example, by what is probably the only surviving specimen of figurative art from the early days of Constantinople—the two porphyry groups commonly called the Tetrarchs in the Piazza of San Marco in Venice. By the end of the fourth century, however, a cultural uplift in the circle of the ruling Theodosian house introduced a short-lived classical revival. A child's sarcophagus discovered at Istanbul in 1933 provides an excellent illustration of that revival. Its long sides are decorated with flying angels—one could as well call them victories—the short sides with standing apostles. The paired angels who hold between them the monogram of Christ show excellent control of foreshortening, and their easy flowing rhythm is appropriately expressed by a style of carving that tends to be slightly blurred. Another beautiful specimen of the same revival is the head of the Emperor Arcadius (395-408) which was discovered at Istanbul in 1949. Its dilated, visionary eyes are a standard trait of the official portraiture of that period, but the expression of the face is benign and an elusive smile plays in the corners of the mouth—a welcome change after the frowning, brutal effigies of the Constantinian emperors.

In the field of major sculpture, it is only through the monuments collected at Istanbul that we can today study the Theodosian revival. The manifestations of this movement were not, however, confined to the capital: they also include the remarkable mosaics of the church of St George at Salonica and the exquisite ivory diptych of the Symmachi and Nicomachi which is of Italian origin and is now divided between the Victoria and Albert Museum in London and the Cluny Museum in Paris. These monuments speak to us of the days when, in spite of the rigors of imperial legislation, Christians and pagans could still mingle in urbane intercourse, when bishops attended pagan schools of philosophy and when avowed pagans could still hold the highest offices of state. It was a truce of short duration; and as we advance into the fifth century this tolerant urbanity disappears.

If we look for a fitting symbol of the fifth century, it is in the land walls of Constantinople that we shall find it. Four miles of a triple rampart, the greatest work of fortification that antiquity has left us, rose to protect the capital against the advancing Goths and Huns. For the next thousand years, after Rome and the western Empire had fallen, these walls were to guard the seat of eastern Christendom.

HEAD OF THE EMPEROR ARCADIUS (395-408). ARCHAEOLOGICAL MUSEUM, ISTANBUL.

MAIN CHURCH OF ALAHAN MANASTIRI, LOOKING EAST. LATE FIFTH CENTURY.

For the development of figurative art in the fifth century a valuable body of material is provided by the mosaic pavements of Antioch. The great abundance of these pavements gives us an opportunity, so rare in other cases, of following step by step the evolution of one particular genre, and this leads us to rather unexpected conclusions. We may note, first of all, a remarkable persistence of the antique figure style, a phenomenon that we shall have occasion to emphasize again in the course of this chapter. Conversely, there is very little oriental influence to be seen, and this in the capital of ancient Syria which has always been considered as the meeting-place of east and west. And yet, in the context of an art that is unmistakably Mediterranean, there appears in the fifth century a new approach to composition that is decidedly unclassical: illusionistic settings disappear and are replaced by a neutral white background on which individual figures are scattered, not indeed at random, but in a fashion that bears no relation to physical reality. The well-known Megalopsychia Hunt (so named after the personification of Magnanimity which occupies its center), a work of the third quarter of the fifth century, illustrates this point. The composition is carefully ordered: longitudinal, transverse and diagonal axes are provided by trees, while hunters and animals are disposed concentrically. Yet this is not the order of nature, and while each figure is realistically observed, the overall effect is one of carpet-like abstraction.

In the field of figural sculpture one may observe in the fifth century a gradual decline from the standard set by the Theodosian age; the pendulum swings back towards a ponderous primitivism. Discouraged by the Church, major sculpture lingers on as an appendage of the imperial cult. The last monument of this kind that has come down to us is the Colossus of Barletta, removed from Constantinople after 1204: it probably represents the Emperor Marcian (450-457). We know from literature that statues of emperors continued to be made until the end of the eighth century, but we do not mourn their loss. Sculpture in the round was dying in the Byzantine world, not to be reborn.

Vital developments, however, were taking place in the realm of architecture. From the Peace of the Church (313) until the early sixth century the standard type of church building in all parts of the Empire was the basilica: an excellent example is provided by the roofless church of St John of Studius at Istanbul (463), and there are even more monumental examples in Asia Minor such as the huge basilica of St Mary at Ephesus or that of St Thekla at Meryamlık. The basilica admitted of numerous variations. Basically, however, it was a barn-like structure covered with a timber roof, and it could attain enormous proportions without posing any difficult problems of engineering. Like the civic basilica from which it was descended, the Christian basilica was essentially a house of assembly. The internal colonnades imparted to it a marked longitudinal axis, while the apse (the only part of the building that normally received an elaborate decoration in mosaic or painting) provided a natural focus of interest. The alternative type of architecture was based on the "centralized" plan, but this—setting aside a few exceptions—was not used for episcopal or parish churches before the early sixth century. It was used for baptisteries, for funeral buildings (and hence for *martyria*, i.e. memorial churches connected with the tombs or relics of martyrs) and also for reception halls in palaces. The subsequent adoption of the centralized plan for ordinary church buildings is a subject that has engendered a great volume of controversy. Was the idea native to the Mediterranean or was it imported from the East? Was the impulsion given by the *martyrium*, the baptistery or the palace hall? Rather than try to answer this academic question it is perhaps more important to note that the centralized and especially the domed church implies a shift in the attitude towards public worship. We are now dealing not so much with the meeting of the Christian community as with a supernatural pageant.

A transitional monument of some interest is Alahan Manastırı situated in the mountainous region of Isauria in southern Turkey. The original name of the monastery is not known, neither is the exact date of its main church, although there is good reason to place it towards the last quarter of the fifth century. In plan, the church of Alahan is, broadly speaking, basilical, but the central space is dominated by a tall rectangular tower. The rectangle is reduced to an octagon by means of corner squinches, thus providing a base for the roof which was not domed or vaulted, as has often been claimed, but surely formed a pyramidal tent of timber. This accounts for the lightness of the entire structure. Even though it was not domed, Alahan Manastırı marks a step in the combination of longitudinal with centralized planning. What is also of interest is that the central part of the nave, i.e. the area under the tower, was screened off by means of parapets and must therefore have been reserved for the liturgical ceremonies. This reflects a trend that may be followed even in the normal basilicas of the eastern provinces: the choir projects more and more into the nave until it occupies the entire center of the building, thus pushing the congregation into the aisles. Once the greater part of the nave had been invaded by the clergy, the basilical plan lost its *raison d'être*.

The culmination of centralized architecture was achieved at Constantinople in the reign of the great Justinian (527-565), and is today represented by two famous buildings, SS. Sergius and Bacchus (Küçük Ayasofya Camii) and St Sophia. St Sergius was built, it would seem, just before Justinian's accession, and is therefore a little earlier than San Vitale at Ravenna, to which it offers a striking resemblance. In plan, St Sergius is an octagon within a square. The dome, built on this octagonal base, is ingeniously subdivided into sixteen slices, alternately flat and concave. Although not very large, the interior produces an effect of extraordinary spaciousness. The horizontal entablature of the lower order upon which, in handsome capital letters, is inscribed a pompous epigram in honor of Justinian and his spouse Theodora, is a "conservative" feature. Otherwise, both carving and architecture show the perfect harmony of a new artistic synthesis. The Corinthian capital which, in the fifth century, still ruled supreme has finally been replaced by the impost capital, better adapted to receive the thrust of arches. Here we see two varieties of the impost capital, the Ionic impost and the

INTERIOR OF ST SOPHIA (532-537), ISTANBUL, LOOKING EAST.

93

"melon," both decorated with carving that has renounced modelling altogether in favor of a white-on-black contrast between the forward plane and the deeply undercut background. The effect produced thereby is like that of lace.

To be a great builder was one of the traditional attributes of the ancient ruler, and Justinian had an uncontrollable passion for building. The chance he needed was provided by a popular uprising (January 532) which reduced the center of Constantinople into a mass of smouldering ruins. The cathedral of St Sophia, Constantine's church of St Irene, the vestibule of the palace, the famous bath of Zeuxippus with its vast collection of ancient statues, and many other notable buildings were burnt down. As soon as the revolt had been quelled, the ground was cleared for rebuilding; hardly a month had passed before work was started on a new and incomparably more splendid cathedral. Less than six years later (537) the immense fabric had been completed.

We know very little concerning the two architects, Anthemius and Isidore, who were entrusted with the erection of the cathedral. Both were natives of Asia Minor and both were also scholars. Anthemius, the senior partner, is reported to have invented some kind of a steam engine by means of which he once played a practical joke on an objectionable neighbor. As a mathematician, he did notable work on conic sections. Isidore was what we would call today a professor of engineering. It would be rash to conclude from this that neither one of them had had any practical experience of architecture; it may be more accurate to say that they combined architectural practice with a high degree of theoretical knowledge. It is, in any case, to Justinian's credit that he engaged men of such calibre instead of a professional master-builder who might have produced a sounder structure, but certainly a much more conventional one. Justinian himself took an active interest in the progress of the work and, we may imagine, made rather a nuisance of himself by interfering with the architects' activities. In later times many legends were woven round the construction of the Great Church. It was said that the design was brought down from heaven by an angel; that ten thousand workmen were employed; that the mortar was made highly adhesive by thinning it, not with water, but with a decoction of barley and elm-bark; that the dome was built of especially light bricks, twelve of which weighed as much as one ordinary brick; that Justinian ran out of funds when the structure had reached gallery level, and that an angel came to his rescue by uncovering hidden treasure; that the altar-table was made by melting together gold and silver, pearls and precious stones, glass, copper and electrum, lead, iron and tin, and casting this amalgam in one slab. These and other stories illustrate the naive amazement that was felt in the Middle Ages before the technical achievements of a richer and more advanced age.

It is now almost impossible to determine the amount of originality shown by the design of St Sophia. All we can say is that whereas several earlier buildings (SS. Sergius and Bacchus among them) display significant affinities with St Sophia, none of them comes sufficiently close to be called a prototype. We should not forget, however, that the surviving buildings represent only a tiny fraction of the entire architectural output of that period. It is entirely possible that the design embodied in St Sophia had been tried out earlier, though, of course, on a smaller scale, and that the exploit of Anthemius and Isidore consisted in applying it to a building of unprecedented scale. Further archaeological discoveries may some day throw new light on this problem.

The design of St Sophia cannot be expressed in a simple sentence, much less by a label such as "domed basilica." To be sure, it combines the longitudinal (basilical) principle with the centralized or radial, but it does so in a singular manner. The ground-plan is in fact nearly square, and the only basilical elements are the division into three aisles and the presence of rectilinear colonnades between the main piers of the dome. The structural skeleton of the building is, however, governed by the dome whose prodigious thrust is neutralized on two sides (east and west), first by semidomes of the same diameter as the main dome, then by smaller exedrae. The two remaining sides, north and south, do not have the same abutment, being filled with straight curtain-walls (tympana), and, as first built, proved to be of insufficient strength. As a result of this flaw, the original dome, which was about twenty feet lower than the present one and a little wider from north to south, collapsed in 563. Thereupon much of the superstructure was dismantled and rebuilt in the form it still retains today. Partial collapses of the second dome in 989 and 1346 were made good without introducing any substantial alterations.

Considering the structural vulnerability of St Sophia and the historical upheavals it has passed through, its state of preservation is nothing short of miraculous. In this respect the Turks deserve much of the credit: having converted St Sophia into their chief mosque, they have kept it in good repair and have refrained from introducing any interior alterations except the bare minimum required by Mohammedan ritual. The slight southward shift in the direction of the altar-niche (to make it face Mecca), the preacher's pulpit, the low platforms for the chanters, even the rather gaudy Sultan's loge which the Swiss architect Fossati contrived in 1847-1849 hardly detract from the total effect of the interior. We have only to think what "improvements," what baroque altars and pre-Raphaelite mosaics would have been inflicted on St Sophia had the church stood in western Europe!

The interior of St Sophia has been variously judged through the ages. In the eighteenth century enlightened Europeans found it disappointing: they were particularly shocked by its unclassical proportions and by the "Gothic" carving of the capitals. Their taste for rationality was more fully satisfied by the imperial mosques. Even Lamartine described St Sophia as a product of corruption and decadence, and it inspired him with "fright, silence and meditation on the instability of human works." As the Romantic movement progressed, however, St Sophia came back into favor. Théophile Gautier

MOSAIC RINCEAU OF ABOUT A.D. 570 IN A ROOM AT THE SOUTHWEST CORNER OF ST SOPHIA, ISTANBUL.

judged it the most perfect church he had ever seen, superior even to Gothic cathedrals —the highest compliment that could have been paid at the time. There is much, of course, in St Sophia that makes a strong appeal to the romantic imagination: an overwhelming majesty that is deeply religious, an exotic richness of decoration, and withal a picturesque irregularity that imparts to the building an illusion of life. Lines curve and bulge, columns lean away from the center, floors undulate. And then there are the eloquent marks left by the passage of time and the succession of religions: the tell-tale cavities caused by the removal of icons and crosses, the patination of bronze and marble, the deep wear of the paving slabs, the indecipherable palimpsest of graffiti upon the walls. Moved as we are by these sights, we must learn to distinguish the original from the added, the intended from the accidental.

Already in the sixth century the historian Procopius made the perceptive remark that the interior of St Sophia seemed to generate its own light. The wonderful play of light is indeed something that immediately strikes the visitor: no window affords a glimpse of the outside world, yet from all directions slanting shafts of light radiate upon the nave. So subtle is the effect, so mysterious the areas of semi-darkness that we feel cheated when we are told that this wonderful illumination has come about partly by historical accident. And yet it is a fact that Justinian's church (as rebuilt after 563, and surely the original church as well) must have admitted considerably more light than at present. In the two great tympana alone the window area was about double what it is today; the windows of the semidomes and of the apse have also been partly blocked up in Turkish times. Whether the ancient glazing was white or colored (as apparently in San Vitale, Ravenna) we have at present no means to judge; we must remember, however, that the original interior also afforded much greater reflection from the vast expanse of gold mosaic than obtains at present from the dull, mustard-colored plaster that covers the greater part of the vaults.

We have alluded to the mosaic decoration, but here we must admit a large part of ignorance. The figural mosaics, of which more will be said later, are all of the ninth and subsequent centuries. The Justinianic decoration has survived in the ceiling of the narthex, in the arches of the nave colonnades and in various subsidiary vaults: it is entirely non-figural. The commonest motifs are scrolls of acanthus, large jewelled crosses, rhombi and stars, sometimes on a gold, sometimes on a dark blue background. In a small room off the south gallery (dating, it would seem, from about 570) is a particularly luxuriant rinceau, the configuration of which offers, incidentally, a close resemblance to the Umayyad mosaics in the Dome of the Rock at Jerusalem. In the center of St Sophia's dome there was originally an enormous mosaic cross. Are we to conclude from this that the Justinianic mosaics of St Sophia were entirely non-figural? This may be too sweeping a view, though it should be observed that the architectural forms of the interior were quite inappropriate to any developed figural decoration. Broadly speaking, we are probably justified in imagining the dome, semidomes, vaults and arches covered with a wealth of abstract decoration on a field of glistening gold.

In reconstructing the original appearance of St Sophia we must also make allowance for the liturgical furnishings: the open chancel-screen of twelve columns, the ciborium over the altar-table, the *synthronon* rising in seven steps within the conch of the apse, and, above all, the monumental pulpit in the center of the nave; the multitude of *polycandela*—perforated lamp-holders, some circular, others cruciform—suspended from the arches and the rim of the dome. All of this *mobilier* was sheathed in silver, decorated with niello and gilding, and must have produced a tremendous glitter. Today, it is only in St Mark's at Venice that we can obtain some faint idea of what a Byzantine church looked like, with its mosaics and furnishings; in St Sophia we must remember that we are looking at an empty shell.

Fortunately, a considerable volume of silver plate dating from the sixth century has come to us. Important finds were made early in this century in Syria and Cyprus, and only a few years ago a cache of unprecedented richness came to light near Finike in southern Turkey, a considerable portion of which is now in the Istanbul Museum

SILVER CENSER DISCOVERED NEAR FINIKE, SECOND HALF OF THE SIXTH CENTURY. ARCHAEOLOGICAL MUSEUM, ISTANBUL.

The cache of silver objects (censer, patens, book-covers, lamps and *polycandela*, sheathing for colonnettes, capitals and architrave etc.) recently found near Finike is probably the most important of its kind in terms of the volume and variety of its contents. Some of the pieces, like the censer illustrated here, bear the name of the bishop Eutychianos who, it may be supposed, ordered a complete set of ecclesiastical silver furnishings at Constantinople. Several other silver treasures, like those of Lampousa in Cyprus (also including a censer which is now in the British Museum), of Hama and Riha in Syria, of Mytilene, etc., consist likewise of objects dating from the sixth or early seventh centuries, and must have been buried for safety under the threat of the first Arab attacks. It was precisely off the coast of Finike that, in 655, the Arabs inflicted a crushing defeat on the Byzantine navy commanded by the Emperor Constans II who barely escaped with his life.

SILVER PATEN DISCOVERED AT STUMA IN SYRIA, A.D. 577-578. ARCHAEOLOGICAL MUSEUM, ISTANBUL.

MOSAIC PAVEMENT OF THE GREAT PALACE, ISTANBUL, END OF THE SIXTH CENTURY OR LATER.

(the rest having been unfortunately dispersed after its discovery). These objects often bear hall-marks which were applied by the central government in Constantinople and which supply exact dates. The interest of these patens, chalices, lamps, censers, etc. is not confined to helping us visualize the *mobilier* of a Byzantine church: they are also a precious guide to the development of Christian iconography and artistic style. Thus, the so-called Stuma paten, which was discovered in northern Syria and dates from the reign of Justin II (565-578), offers one of the earliest known representations of the Communion of the Apostles. Note the duplication of the figure of Christ so as to make him simultaneously dispense the bread and the wine to the approaching apostles, a peculiarity that was to persist in Orthodox Christian painting for the next thousand years. The style of the paten is rather harsh and linear, the faces have long noses and big staring eyes—characteristics which art historians of the last generation used to associate with the art of Syria. Judging by the hall-marks, however, the Stuma paten appears to have been made at Constantinople. On the beautiful silver censer from the Finike treasure is a series of episodes relating to the Nativity of Christ, and the same are repeated, with the addition of the Miracles, on two identical gold amulettes of the sixth century, discovered at Adana and now also in the Istanbul Museum.

Justinian's grandiose attempt to reconstitute the empire of Augustus was not destined to succeed. The structure he erected began to crack even before he died. His successors struggled valiantly to shore it up, but to no avail: the collapse was catastrophic. While Italy fell to the Lombards, the entire Balkan peninsula was overrun by Slavs and Avars. There followed an epic war against the traditional enemy, the Persians; the great Emperor Heraclius had hardly time to subdue the Sasanian Empire when a new force, the Arabs, fired by Mohammed's religion, broke into the Mediterranean world. Within the span of one generation the entire world-order of antiquity was irrevocably altered. The Persian Empire vanished, Egypt, Syria and Palestine were lost to the Arabs, the Caliph ruled at Damascus while his lieutenants were subduing the North African coast, battering their way into the Caucasus and pushing the Byzantines into the highlands of Asia Minor. By the early eighth century the Arabs had reached the Atlantic. In 717 they were, for the second time, besieging Constantinople.

For about a century after the death of Justinian artistic traditions were somehow maintained. The antique heritage—call it hellenism or classicism—lingered on, at any rate in the upper class of society. We can trace this survival most clearly in the silver plate, some of it still decorated with subjects drawn from allegory or Greek mythology, which continued to be made until the reign of Constans II (641-668). An important monument illustrating this trend is the mosaic pavement of the Great Palace of Constantinople. Discovered in 1935, this pavement has since been the subject of much controversy among scholars. It formed part of a monumental complex consisting of a peristyle court that gave access to some kind of a ceremonial hall. The court measures about 213 by 180 feet, and the mosaic, which is nearly thirty-three feet wide, formed

PARAPET SLAB REPRESENTING A PEACOCK, NINTH OR TENTH CENTURY. ARCHAEOLOGICAL MUSEUM, ISTANBUL.

Between the eighth century and the second half of the twelfth sculpture in the round was entirely absent from the Byzantine world. Its place was taken by ornamental carving. In churches carving was lavished on the chancel screen, on capitals, parapet slabs, door frames and on the cornice that normally made the round of the interior at the level of the springing of the arches. The relief is always very shallow and the effect two-dimensional. The repertoire of motifs includes a wide range of geometric and vegetal ornament as well as stylized animals. Individually, these motifs are usually traceable to the Mediterranean art of the fifth and sixth centuries, but they have been re-interpreted according to the dictates of medieval taste: Lombard reliefs of the seventh and eighth centuries achieve similar results without approaching the elegance of Byzantine work. In evaluating the aesthetic effect of Byzantine carving, we should not forget, however, that originally it was painted in contrasting colors and that the projecting elements might even have been gilded.

Few surviving Byzantine churches have retained their carved ornament *in situ*. When churches were converted into mosques, the chancel screen and other furnishings appropriate to Christian worship were naturally removed. It is only exceptionally—as, for example, in the Monastery of Lips (Fenari Isa Camii) of the early tenth century at Istanbul—that the abundance of preserved carvings enables us to reconstitute the original decoration with some accuracy. The two matching pieces reproduced here were found at Istanbul. They probably formed the closure slabs of a chancel screen.

a continuous border along all four sides of the court. The subject-matter is rural and evokes a mood of poetic romanticism. An endless array of little scenes—hunting, fishing, children playing, a nursing mother, a variety of wild and domestic animals—are loosely arranged in three parallel zones against a uniform white background. Trees and rocks, placed at irregular intervals, serve as punctuation marks. The execution of the individual motifs is admirably free and elegant, the range of colors rich and subtle. At first glance the pavement appears so antique that some scholars have wished to date it in the third or fourth century A.D. In fact, archaeological evidence has shown that it cannot be earlier than the end of the sixth, and a late dating is supported by the casual composition of the mosaic which could be conceived as going on endlessly, governed only by a horizontal rhythm.

The survival of classicism at Constantinople until the great collapse of the mid-seventh century explains a great deal in the later development of Byzantine art. We should not, however, place undue stress on this fact: the classicism in question had already become fossilized. It was confined to the orbit of the imperial court and was becoming more and more widely separated from the main current of art which was finding expression in the service of religion. From about the mid-sixth century onward the leading place in both art and religious devotion came to be occupied by the icon.

PARAPET SLAB REPRESENTING A PEACOCK, NINTH OR TENTH CENTURY. ARCHAEOLOGICAL MUSEUM, ISTANBUL.

When we speak of the icon, we use the term in a restricted sense which is derived more from Russian than from Greek usage; for in Greek *eikon* has always meant any kind of image, not necessarily that of a holy personage painted on a panel. Medieval legend would have us believe that the tradition of icon painting was as old as Christianity and that it was instituted by St Luke, but this is very far from the truth. In fact, the early Church, anxious above all to maintain the spirituality of its worship and to dissociate itself from idolatry, expressly repudiated every form of sacred portraiture. We do not have to explain here by what slow degrees the art of representation established itself in the Church. In the fourth and fifth centuries the material focus of Christian veneration was provided by the tombs and relics of martyrs. It is only after Justinian that the icon, the sacred portrait, attains exceptional prominence as an object of popular worship.

The purpose of the icon determined its artistic form. This purpose was not simply symbolic or instructive. To an ordinary Byzantine of the post-Justinianic period the icon became more and more identified with the person it represented, its "prototype." The relationship between image and prototype was no longer a matter of external resemblance, but became, so to speak, essential and supernatural. Saints were regarded as dwelling in their icons and acting through them; icons worked miracles, spoke, bled when stabbed. The icon, therefore, had to represent the actual presence of the saint, and the most effective way of doing so was by means of a portrait, frontal and immobile, intense and hypnotic in expression, and stripped of all inessentials. For this purpose there was a tradition ready at hand, and this was the anti-classical, "sub-antique" tradition.

The original opposition to image-worship was not, however, dead in the Church. When, by the beginning of the eighth century, the Christian Empire had all but collapsed, when the Arabs were standing before Constantinople, the same question must have been on everyone's mind: for what enormous sins were the faithful being chastised? The Old Testament provided the answer: had not the Israelites, too (the prototype of the Christian people), been similarly chastised when they went a-whoring after idolatry, and had not Moses laid down the immutable law, "Thou shalt not make unto thee a graven image, nor the likeness of any form that is in heaven above, or that is in the earth beneath"?

The Emperor who, in 717, repulsed the Arabs from Constantinople, Leo III, inspired and aided by a group of Anatolian bishops, resolved to banish the use of images from Christian worship. The prohibition was enacted in 730 and remained in force until 787. It was revived for the second time in 814 (once more after a disastrous Byzantine defeat, this time by the Bulgarians) and was finally repealed in 843. The century of Iconoclasm represents for us the most obscure period of Byzantine art. We know from documents that the iconoclast emperors did not outlaw every kind of human

MOSAIC OF THE ARCHANGEL GABRIEL, PROBABLY A.D. 867. ST SOPHIA, ISTANBUL.

CHURCH OF ST IRENE, ISTANBUL, INTERIOR LOOKING EAST. BUILT BY JUSTINIAN AFTER 532, UPPER PORTIONS REBUILT AFTER 740.

representation: secular art was maintained and compositions glorifying the emperor particularly encouraged. Yet the sphere of secular art had by this time become so restricted that the ban on religious representation must have had a sweeping effect.

It is worth reflecting that western European art was in the eighth century practically restricted to abstract ornament and that, beyond the confines of Byzantium, lay the Mohammedan world where the representation of every living being was prohibited. All the way from Ireland to Persia the tradition of human portrayal seemed to be on the verge of extinction.

Among the very few surviving specimens of iconoclast art is the apse mosaic in the church of St Irene at Constantinople. This ancient church, founded by Constantine and rebuilt by Justinian, was partly destroyed by an earthquake in 740 and reconstructed a few years later when, it would seem, the mosaic was also made. Against a pale gold background stands, in stark simplicity, a black cross on a stepped base. The cross, symbol of Christian victory, was the favorite emblem of the iconoclast emperors. In other churches, as we know from documents, they replaced images of saints with representations of trees, vegetal scrolls and different kinds of birds, thus converting God's house into a vegetable garden and an aviary, to use the words of a contemporary author. The mosaics of the mosque at Damascus (early eighth century) give us an adequate picture of what these Byzantine decorations must have looked like.

The iconoclast controversy generated an amount of passionate involvement that is difficult for us to share. Starting as a reform of ritual, it soon developed into a profound Christological issue. It was on the possibility of representing Christ that the argument was increasingly focused. For if Christ could not be portrayed, it followed that he had not been fully a man, that the Incarnation had not been real: so argued the iconophile party which stood for the majority of the population. When, at length, the iconoclasts were ousted from power, there was a widespread feeling that the ultimate heresy had been defeated and that the Church had attained its ideal perfection. The faith, as defined by the Councils, was henceforth to remain immutable: nothing could be added to it, nothing taken away.

While drawing upon themselves the execration of the pious, the iconoclast emperors had saved the Empire from collapse. The Arabs were pushed back to the Taurus mountains and, at the end of the eighth century, the Byzantines began to regain from the Slavs their Balkan possessions. The Empire in 843 was based very solidly on Asia Minor. It was a compact state with a tightly knit military organization; a state dominated by two racial stocks, Armenian and Slav, yet Greek-speaking and totally committed to the Byzantine ideal of a single Christian Empire. Now that the Arab menace had receded, the Byzantine government felt strong enough to extend, whether by military force, diplomacy or missionary work, the sphere of its authority.

THE EMPEROR JOHN II COMNENUS AND THE EMPRESS IRENE MAKING OFFERINGS TO THE VIRGIN AND CHILD. 1122 OR A LITTLE LATER. MOSAIC IN THE GALLERY OF ST SOPHIA, ISTANBUL.

The re-hellenization of Greece, the conversion to Byzantine Christianity first of the Bulgarian, and later of the nascent Russian state were the chief and permanent achievements of this glorious period.

It was roughly from 850 to 1050 that the medieval Byzantine Empire stood at its height. The same period plus about a century (say down to 1150) represents the "classical" age of Byzantine art, an art that expressed itself most fully in the realm of religious painting and particularly of mosaic. Among the masterpieces of this art, the figural mosaics of St Sophia occupy a leading place: the Madonna and archangel in the apse (most probably of the year 867), the panel above the Imperial Door and the three surviving bishops in the north tympanum (end of the ninth century), the portrait of the Emperor Alexander (912-913), the panel of the southwest vestibule (probably of the late tenth century), the portraits of the Empress Zoe and her third husband, Constantine IX Monomachus (between 1028 and 1042), and those of John II, his wife Irene and his son Alexius (shortly after 1122). We have here a chronological series which invites us to look for differences between these works and to trace an evolutionary curve.

Differences, to be sure, may be found, and yet it is the similarity of these various mosaics that immediately strikes the eye. What they have in common, first of all, is the elimination of picture space. The figures are placed on a plain gold background. In some cases there is no ground-line at all, while in others the figures stand on a green strip, but even this produces no illusion of depth. The strip of ground usually consists of three parallel ribbons, the topmost one being the darkest and the bottom one the lightest; as a result of this anti-illusionistic device, the ground does not appear to recede, but forms instead a stratified vertical parapet in front of which the figures are suspended. The second common element of the mosaics we have enumerated is the absence of a uniform source of light. Figures cast no shadows, while the shading of the figures themselves and of the accessory furniture (thrones and footstools) is applied indiscriminately, sometimes on one side, sometimes on the other. Thirdly, all of the above mosaics have the same imperturbable and motionless serenity, even when the subject-matter implies movement. The compositions are built up symmetrically by a process of juxtaposition and without any real *rapport* between the figures represented. Take, for example, the panel above the Imperial Door. Whatever its deeper significance, it represents an emperor (presumably Leo VI) prostrating himself before an enthroned Christ. In addition to these two personages, there are two balancing busts enclosed in circular medallions: the Virgin Mary on the left, an angel or archangel on the right. In terms of content, the mosaic portrays an action involving several figures: the kneeling emperor pays homage to his celestial overlord, the Virgin Mary presumably intercedes on the emperor's behalf, while the angel stands guard. There is, however, nothing to bind these figures together. Christ looks straight ahead without appearing to pay any attention either to his Mother or to the emperor; the angel, too, looks ahead or even slightly away from the center of action; while both the Virgin Mary and the emperor appear to be staring at some object placed at 45 degrees to the plane of the picture. One could make similar observations concerning all the other mosaics of St Sophia that include several figures.

These compositional constants, coupled with the immutability of iconographic types, produced an art which, broadly speaking, stood still for several centuries: the perfect expression of a faith to which nothing could be added and from which nothing could be taken away. It is only in the greater or lesser plasticity of the figures, in the modelling of the faces, in the disposition of the drapery and the use of this or that kind of ornament that an evolution can be traced. Within the entire "middle Byzantine" period, i.e. from the middle of the ninth century to the middle of the twelfth, the general trend is from relative freedom towards an ever-growing academicism and desiccation. Take one of the earlier mosaics of this group, say the splendid archangel in the apse of St Sophia. Although not fully rounded, he is remarkably statuesque. The white silk of his mantle falls in heavy, shiny folds. The face which has an aristocratic, almost supercilious appearance, shades off delicately from a milky white to pink. There is not a harsh line anywhere. The panel above the Imperial Door, which may be some twenty or thirty years later than the archangel, is the work of a lesser master. The drapery is a little fussy, the figures rather heavily proportioned. Even so, it is a robust work, and the very unevenness of the execution imparts some life to it. When, however, we come to the mosaic of the southwest vestibule, we can see that academicism has already set in. The workmanship has become more regular, the modelling of the faces more rigid. In the imperial portraits of the south gallery the style has hardened even further. Encased in their bejewelled carapaces, the emperors and empresses seem to be incapable of movement. The faces are modelled by means of tightly packed rows of cubes. Instead of juxtaposing patches and dots of contrasting colors, the artist now arranges cubes of the same color to produce lines of tension after the manner of a contour map.

In analysing Byzantine mosaics of the "classical" period, it is almost inevitable that we should begin by making negative statements, for their style can most conveniently be defined by the absence of some of those conventions or devices that make for illusionistic representation (spatial recession, single-source illumination, lifelike grouping of figures, etc.). What then is it that makes these mosaics such great works of art? We can suggest at least two answers: first, a splendid use of color and light; second, the appropriateness of the style to the medium.

The reflection of light is a prime consideration in all mosaic work. Byzantine artists of the "classical" period used both glass and stone tesserae, i.e. they had to combine a reflecting material with a mat material. The most brilliant tesserae were the gold and

The art of cloisonné enamel on gold reached a peak at Constantinople between the ninth and the twelfth centuries. Since not a single noteworthy specimen of this art has remained in Turkey, we reproduce the famous Limburg reliquary which is not only one of the finest works of its kind, but offers the further advantage of being exactly dated. It is in the form of a rectangular box with a sliding lid. The relic itself is contained in a cross with double traverse for which a cavity has been fashioned in the interior of the box. The cross is dated by an inscription to the joint reign of Constantine VII and Romanus II (945-959), while the box was made soon after 963 at the behest of Basil Proedros, natural son of the Emperor Romanus I. A knight of the Fourth Crusade, one Heinrich von Uelmen, brought the object from Constantinople to Germany in 1208.

The enamel decoration of the box consists of an assemblage of little plaques. Those on the lid represent the Deesis, the twelve apostles and eight saints; those of the interior the hierarchy of angels. Small particles of further highly venerated relics, such as the Crown of Thorns and the Sponge, the girdle of the Virgin Mary and the hair of St John the Baptist, were contained between the arms of the cross.

GOLD AND ENAMEL RELIQUARY OF THE TRUE CROSS, MIDDLE OF THE TENTH CENTURY. CATHEDRAL TREASURY OF LIMBURG-ON-THE-LAHN.

THE EMPEROR ROMANUS II AND THE EMPRESS EUDOCIA CROWNED BY CHRIST, 945-949. IVORY PLAQUE.
BIBLIOTHÈQUE NATIONALE, PARIS.

silver ones (made by attaching gold or silver leaf on a glass base); next in reflecting power came the pigmented glasses (blue, green, red, etc.), then the marbles (white, grey and pink), finally the soft stones and chips of terracotta. Since the cubes were pressed individually into a layer of moist plaster, every Byzantine mosaic has an uneven surface which breaks up the reflection and produces a *chatoiement* that constantly changes with the illumination. In the case of the gold backgrounds the Byzantine artists knew very well that an even expanse of gold would have looked unbearably "brassy" and would have submerged the figural compositions; to prevent this from happening they often mixed silver cubes among the gold ones, and they also controlled the glitter by tilting the cubes at an angle.

Color and light cannot, therefore, be separated in discussing Byzantine mosaics; but even if we set aside the peculiar effects of reflection, what a wonderful palette do these mosaics have! It would be difficult to match in the entire history of art color effects so rich and yet so subtly harmonious. Consider once again the archangel in the apse of St Sophia: here whites, greys and bluish greens predominate, the opalescent hues of the mantle being echoed (because the same materials are used) in the majestic wings. This subdued color scheme is, however, heightened by patches of gold—note the diagonal *tablion* cutting across the marble like a shaft of sunlight—and upon the gold are fold-lines and delicate patterns in a deep red.

It is rather more difficult to explain why it is that the medium of mosaic is so admirably suited to the "classical" Byzantine style. While it is true that mosaic work is a kind of painting, it differs from normal painting in some important respects: the range of tones is more limited, the material more obtrusive. By reducing the size of the cubes and the interstices between them, it is possible to approximate more and more the effect of painting, but no matter how ingenious such attempts may be, they are inevitably false to the genre of mosaic. In general, it may be said that the more

To illustrate the art of Byzantine ivory-carvers we must, once again, look outside Turkey. The Romanus ivory is a particularly important object both because of its high artistic merit and because it provides a basis for the chronology of numerous other ivories of similar style that are undated. The emperor represented has previously been identified as Romanus IV (1068-1071), but is now considered to be Romanus II. Born in 938, Romanus II was married in 944 to Bertha (renamed Eudocia), illegitimate daughter of Hugh, king of Italy. She died five years later, still a child. The ivory may have been made in 945 when Romanus was crowned co-emperor by his father. By a common convention, he and his wife are represented not as small children but fully grown. Christ's statuesque figure provides an excellent example of the classicizing spirit that prevailed at the court of Constantinople in the ninth and tenth centuries. As is also the case with the Carolingian Renascence, this spirit found expression mostly in costly works of the minor arts such as ivory carvings and illuminated manuscripts.

naturalistic or illusionistic a mosaic attempts to be, the more it fails. The art of mural mosaic poses certain requirements: it demands a scale that is sufficiently monumental, an adequate distance from the beholder, and a manner or style that is sufficiently abstract for the texture of the materials and the play of light to come into their own.

We have dwelt at some length on the figural mosaics of St Sophia because they are the most perfect representatives of Byzantine pictorial art on Turkish soil. They have, however, this important limitation that they relate very badly to the building in which they are placed. The scale of St Sophia is so vast that the figural mosaics are dwarfed by the architecture. Even the figures in the apse, which are three times life size, appear insignificant when viewed from the ground. Now, the fundamental quality of "classical" Byzantine mosaics is that they were conceived as part of an entire church interior and not as individual tableaux: to see this one ought to visit Hosios Loukas or Daphni in Greece. The typical Byzantine church of this period was of modest size, and its interior disposition was usually cruciform or octagonal. The vertical surface of the walls was largely reveted with colored marble and was delimited by a cornice at the springing of the vaults. The mosaics came above the cornice—in the dome, the pendentives, the semidome of the apse, the barrel vaults of the cross-arms. As a result, the figures occupied surfaces that were mostly curved, and they were composed spatially, i.e. with reference to the empty space in front of them and between them. Taken collectively, the mosaic decoration of a Byzantine church formed a "closed system," a miniature Christian universe arranged in a strict order: Christ Pantocrator ruling from the apex of the dome, the Old Testament prophets between the windows of the drum, the Evangelists in the four pendentives upholding, as it were, the structure of salvation by their writings, the Virgin Mary in the apse escorted by angels, the Church Fathers standing behind the altar-table as if taking part in the liturgy, and so on. This mutual interdependence of the mosaic figures explains the elimination of picture space: for when an individual tableau produces the illusion of its own spatial setting, it breaks up the self-contained unity of the church and becomes, as it were, a window opening into another world. Without pressing the comparison too far, it may be helpful to think of "classical" Byzantine mosaics not so much as flat pictures, but as statues arranged in a certain order within the shell of a church.

The above remarks apply to metropolitan monuments. The evolution of figurative art in Byzantine Asia Minor is known to us largely through the rock churches of Cappadocia where we come in contact with rather a different world. Rock churches are scattered all over the territory of Turkey, but it is mostly in the region southwest of Kayseri, around Ürgüp and Niğde that these churches have preserved a large body of mural decoration. The earlier frescoes, of the ninth and tenth centuries, are more akin to Syria than to the Byzantine capital. Very curious from the viewpoint of iconography, these frescoes are usually deployed in continuous friezes, row upon row. Their purpose is to tell a story in comic-strip fashion. The style is primitive, the lines

SCENES FROM THE LIFE OF CHRIST, CHURCH OF TOKALI, GÖREME (CAPPADOCIA). LATE NINTH OR EARLY TENTH CENTURY.

harsh and angular, the figures are pressed close to one another, color is applied in flat local patches. The Byzantine offensive against the Arabs in the latter part of the tenth century—an offensive which overshot the frontier formed by the Taurus mountains and extended Byzantine domination to Antioch and Aleppo—produced an influx of Constantinopolitan currents into the hitherto isolated art of Cappadocia. More elaborate, columnar churches now make their appearance. Strip decoration is banished and replaced by the metropolitan system of isolating certain key episodes of the Biblical story and subordinating these to a hierarchical arrangement. Colors become more varied, attitudes more dignified and theatrical. Even so, provincial naïveté is everywhere apparent: in the clumsy drawing, in the superabundance of ornament, in the unsophisticated brightness of the color scheme.

Further east, round Lake Van and in the foothills of the Caucasus, lay the Armenian and Georgian buffer states which often played an ambiguous role between Byzantium and Islam, and whence the Empire drew so many of its soldiers and military leaders. Here a distinctive art grew up which cannot be treated merely as a provincial variant of Byzantine art. Its main achievement was in the realm of architecture. Building in massive ashlar, the Armenians developed from the seventh century onward a wide variety of domed designs which, by the tenth century, had assumed forms unknown to Byzantine architects. The cathedral of Ani, built by the architect Trdat between 989 and 1001, while following the Byzantine scheme of the cross inscribed in a rectangle, has clustered piers and pointed arches which anticipate by about a century the

CHURCH OF ST GREGORY AT ANI (ARMENIA), A.D. 1215.

The flowering of Armenian architecture in the tenth and early eleventh centuries was interrupted, first by the Byzantine annexation of the country, then by the Seljuk conquest (1064). A further period of intense building activity took place when, a century later, Armenia came under Georgian rule and was brought to a close by the Mongol invasion of the 1240s. This last phase of Armenian architecture is exemplified by the church of St Gregory at Ani, built by a rich merchant, Tigran Honents. Unlike other Armenian buildings of this time which are strongly influenced by Seljuk art, the church of St Gregory reverts to such older models as the cathedrals of Ani and Marmashen (1029). A new spirit is, however, apparent in the slenderer proportions and more abundant ornament. A rich belt of carving fills the spandrels of the blind arcading on all sides of the exterior, while the interior is extensively painted in fresco, perhaps the work of Georgian masters.

CHURCH OF THE HOLY CROSS, AGHT'AMAR (LAKE VAN), BETWEEN 915 AND 921. WEST FAÇADE.

appearance of similar forms in the Gothic West. This poses a problem to which no satisfactory answer has yet been given. We may be hesitant to ascribe too far-reaching an influence to the Armenian school of architecture, but its impact on Byzantine buildings need not surprise us: we refer in particular to that elongation of proportions, to the heightening of the cupola drums, to the articulation of façades by means of blind arcading, to the stepped or clustered pilasters—features common in Armenia, and which begin to invade Byzantine architecture from the tenth century onward.

Building as they did in stone, the Armenians also developed a tradition of ornamental carving to a degree of elaboration never achieved by the Byzantines. The outstanding monument in this respect is the church of Aght'amar built by King Gagik on an island of Lake Van between the years 915 and 921. The façades of this church are covered with a profusion of figural and ornamental work in shallow relief: the King, in ceremonial robes, offering to Christ the model of his church, episodes from the Old Testament, various saints, fantastic animals, "animated" vine scrolls, etc. When seen at close quarters, the execution of the reliefs is rather schematic and crude, but from a distance they produce an effect of exotic richness which contrasts with the bleak, rocky landscape of the island. As with Armenian architecture, here, too, the comparisons that come to mind take us beyond the Byzantine sphere: we are made to think of the twelfth-century churches of Vladimir and Suzdal in Russia and of western Romanesque cathedrals.

The end of the eleventh century marks the breakup of Byzantine rule in Asia Minor. Overrunning Armenia, defeating the Byzantine forces at the battle of Manzikert (1071), the Seljuk Turks reached within the next decade the shores of the Aegean. Their simultaneous conquest of Palestine precipitated the First Crusade. At this point the Byzantine Empire enters a new phase, a phase of renewed if generally unfriendly contact with the Latin West. After centuries of mutual separation, the West emerges as more advanced, more vigorous, more enterprising than the Byzantine East. Norman knights and Venetian merchants come to Constantinople as colonial exploiters. The Levant is born.

The effect of these changes on Byzantine art does not appear to have been immediate. The portraits in St Sophia of John II Comnenus and his Hungarian wife Irene have a jewel-like and rather lifeless precision, a rigidity of modelling which develop but do not alter the style of the Zoe panel. In the illuminated manuscripts of the first half of the twelfth century no new departures are noticeable. The Gospel book of the Greek Patriarchate at Istanbul (Treasury, No. 3) is a typical specimen of the period: it has the simplified, hieratic compositions, the elegant if stiffly drawn figures that are more appropriate to monumental painting, and withal a wealth of enamel-like ornament. The more famous Octateuch of the Seraglio Library, although executed for a member of the imperial family, Isaac Comnenus the brother of John II (died c. 1152), and in

THE DEESIS AND EVANGELISTS, GOSPEL BOOK OF THE FIRST HALF OF THE TWELFTH CENTURY.
GREEK PATRIARCHATE, ISTANBUL.

spite of its undeniable importance for Old Testament iconography, is rather disappointing as a work of art. Its hundreds of miniatures, all of small format, never rise above the level of a mediocre copy. At about the same time a new genre makes its appearance, that of the portable mosaic. The icon of the Virgin Hodegetria in the Greek Patriarchate of Istanbul is one of the earliest and largest (33½ by 23½ inches) representatives of this group. Now, a portable mosaic was simply an *objet de luxe*, a reproduction in a more expensive and time-consuming medium of what could be better done in paint. We are not surprised, therefore, to find in the Virgin Hodegetria, as in most other specimens of the genre, an impersonal finish, a glossiness worthy of Bond Street.

THE MIRACLE AT CANA, ABOUT 1250. FRESCO IN ST SOPHIA, TREBIZOND.

The church of St Sophia at Trebizond was probably founded by the Emperor Manuel I (1238-1263) whose painted portrait, now no longer extant, was seen there in the middle of the last century by George Finlay. Although Manuel was the vassal first of the Seljuks and then of the Mongols, he apparently styled himself on this portrait "Emperor and Autocrat of the Romans," i.e. by the title of the Byzantine emperor. The painted decoration of St Sophia, unfortunately rather damaged, has recently been cleaned by a British expedition and provides a valuable link between the style of the Comnenian period and that of the Palaeologan. The origin of this transitional art is as yet obscure. Should it be sought at Constantinople at the very end of the twelfth century or at Nicaea which, between 1204 and 1261, was the main center of Byzantine culture? The total absence of paintings that may be connected with the kingdom of Nicaea prevents us from charting accurately the development of Byzantine representational art during this particularly interesting period. It is, at any rate, clear that many of the features that have been considered peculiar to the mature Palaeologan style of the early fourteenth century were already present in the Byzantine world about a hundred years earlier and should not, therefore, be ascribed to the influence of the Italian Duecento.

CENTRAL BAY OF THE NARTHEX, ST SOPHIA, TREBIZOND, ABOUT 1250.

THE INFANT VIRGIN FONDLED BY HER PARENTS AND HER PRESENTATION TO THE HIGH PRIESTS.
VAULT MOSAIC IN THE INNER NARTHEX OF KAHRIYE CAMII (ST SAVIOUR IN THE CHORA), ISTANBUL, ABOUT 1315.

It is a great pity that we should not have before us a single work of monumental painting produced at Constantinople in the last quarter of the twelfth century. Indirect evidence from outlying regions, from Sicily (Monreale), Macedonia, Cyprus and Russia, forces us to assume that it was at Constantinople that a new departure in art was made some twenty or thirty years before the sack of the city by the Crusaders (1204), and that this departure consisted in the partial rediscovery of picture space, in a quickening of rhythm and a baroque swirling of drapery. The new style had barely time to establish itself, however, when Constantinople fell and the Byzantine world was fragmented. Three Greek principalities now grew up, one at Nicaea, the second in the Epirus, the third at Trebizond, while the remainder of the Byzantine lands were parcelled out among the Venetians and the feudal lords of the Crusade. We may imagine that the artists of the capital were dispersed and sought employment at the various Orthodox courts of Asia Minor and the Balkans, including those of Bulgaria and Serbia.

The greatest monuments of thirteenth-century Byzantine painting are now in Yugoslavia (Mileševo, Sopoćani). In Turkey—pending further discoveries—we have only the recently cleaned frescoes of St Sophia at Trebizond dating from about 1250. The building is a potpourri of heterogeneous influences: while the fabric is in the Byzantine tradition, the figural carving on the south porch reminds us of Armenian and Georgian decorations; elsewhere are stalactites and rosettes of purely Seljuk workmanship, and there are certain details, such as quatrefoil windows, that must have come from western Europe. The frescoes, however, are purely Byzantine. Without achieving the nobility of Sopoćani, they combine monumental proportions and the rather emphatic modelling of the previous century with a multiplication of picturesque detail. The agitated manner of about 1200 survives in the angel of the Annunciation who rushes towards Mary in such a welter of fluttering drapery as if a violent hurricane were blowing in his face. Elsewhere, for example in the Miracle of Cana, we encounter the architectural backdrop with oblique projections, the draped *vela* which are such a characteristic feature of Palaeologan painting.

In 1261 Constantinople was reconquered from the Latins by the Greek emperor of Nicaea, Michael VIII Palaeologus. Under the rule of his descendants Byzantium was to survive for another two centuries. Although we speak of the Empire of the Palaeologi, this was no more than a small state, internally exhausted, oppressed by its own feudal nobility, exploited by the merchants of Venice and Genoa. Pressed by the Serbians in Europe and the nascent power of the Ottoman Turks in Asia Minor, by 1350 the Byzantine state barely extended from Constantinople to Salonica; by 1400 it was limited to Constantinople itself, part of the Peloponnese and a few Aegean islands. By 1461 every parcel of Byzantine territory had been absorbed by the Turks.

Given this depressing political picture, it is surprising that the Palaeologan state should have produced an art of any note. Yet its artistic achievement—at any rate in painting—was not only of a high calibre, but also very copious, so that decorations in the Palaeologan style are preserved in great numbers. It is, indeed, one of the few phases of Byzantine art that we are able to study with some fullness.

In Constantinople itself the earliest extant Palaeologan work would seem to be the monumental Deesis in the south gallery of St Sophia. The composition is traditional—an enthroned Christ flanked by the figures of the Virgin Mary and John the Baptist—and the background is plain gold, though the cubes are arranged in a fan-like pattern.

FUNERARY CHAPEL OF FETHIYE CAMII (ST MARY PAMMACARISTOS), ISTANBUL, ABOUT 1310.
EXTERIOR FROM THE EAST.

The pareclesion (side chapel) of St Mary Pammacaristos was built as a memorial to a distinguished general, Michael Glabas Tarchaniotes, who died shortly before 1310. The exterior exemplifies the features of later Byzantine architecture: multiplication of little domes, articulation of façades by means of blind arcading, the arrangement of bricks to form decorative patterns. The interior, which is of the four-column type, is among the best preserved in Turkey. The mosaics follow the familiar scheme with minor variations: Christ Pantocrator surrounded by prophets in the dome, an enthroned Christ (instead of the Virgin) in the apse, representations of the major feasts (only the Baptism remains) and figures of individual saints.

FUNERARY CHAPEL OF FETHIYE CAMII (ST MARY PAMMACARISTOS), ISTANBUL, ABOUT 1310. INTERIOR LOOKING SOUTHEAST.

The Deesis mosaic is not dated, and there are some scholars who consider it a work of the twelfth century, in our opinion incorrectly. What strikes us here, first of all, is a mood of almost sentimental sadness. Christ is gentle and pensive, not the angry, authoritarian God we find, for example, at Daphni. Examining the mosaic more closely, we notice that the tesserae are smaller than usual and that the technique is basically that of the brush. The faces are not modelled by means of the tense contour lines of Comnenian art; instead, they shade off imperceptibly in hundreds of curving "strokes." Another surprise: for the first time in Byzantine art we find a cast shadow on Christ's neck. Small as these innovations may be, they infuse a new spirit into an old iconographic formula. We may even wonder whether the patterned background was not inspired by the use of tooled and gilded gesso which, under western influence, began to appear in Byzantine icons of the thirteenth century.

Passing over the much faded frescoes of the Martyrion of St Euphemia which appear to be of the end of the thirteenth century, we reach the mature phase of Palaeologan art in the side-chapel of Fethiye Camii (St Mary Pammacaristos) of about 1310, and especially in Kahriye Camii (St Saviour of the Chora) of about 1315. Of these two monuments Kahriye Camii is incomparably the richer in the extent and variety of its decoration, and we shall therefore confine our comments to it.

We know a great deal about the patron who was responsible for the decoration of Kahriye Camii: he was Theodore Metochites (1270-1332), author, polymath, amateur astronomer and statesman who held the posts of finance minister and later of prime minister until a revolution toppled him from power and sent him into exile. Metochites acquired immense wealth from the exercise of his public duties and, while serving as finance minister (i.e. before 1321), he did what was expected of a man of his position: he endowed a monastery. Instead of setting up a new establishment, however, he chose an existing monastery, that of the Chora, which had the advantage of proximity to the emperor's palace. The Chora had been founded in the sixth century, if not earlier, but the church building was of the eleventh or twelfth, and Metochites did not rebuild it. He added various galleries and chapels to the old church and then proceeded to decorate the entire complex as lavishly as possible. We do not know anything about the artists he employed, but we can be sure that they were the best that money could buy.

The greater part of the surviving decoration is today concentrated in the inner and the outer narthex as well as in a mortuary chapel built against the south side of the church; the decoration of the nartheces is in mosaic, that of the chapel in fresco. The multiplicity of the subjects represented (this is a typical feature of Palaeologan art) prevents us from enumerating them in detail. Suffice it to say that the mosaics narrate first the life of the Virgin on the basis of the apocryphal Protoevangelium of James, and then that of Christ down to the miracles, but excluding the Passion which must have been represented in the church proper. As for the funeral chapel, it contains not

THE HARROWING OF HELL, FRESCO IN THE APSE OF THE FUNERARY CHAPEL, KAHRIYE CAMII
(ST SAVIOUR OF THE CHORA), ISTANBUL, ABOUT 1315.

only subjects appropriate to death and resurrection (the stupendous Harrowing of Hell in the apse and the Last Judgment in the vault), but also a "typological" cycle made up of episodes of the Old Testament that were believed to foreshadow the advent of the Virgin Mary and the Incarnation.

The range of subjects represented in Kahriye Camii is thus incomparably fuller than in a typical church of the "classical" period. Since, moreover, Kahriye Camii is a fairly small building, there inevitably results pictorial overcrowding. If, by an effort of the imagination, we try to reconstruct the original appearance of the interior by completing the missing mosaics and incrustations; if we remember that much of the marble-work was gilded and painted, and that (as recent investigations have shown) there was stained glass in the windows; if we further supply the missing furniture—the iconostasis, the candlesticks, oil lamps, lecterns, etc.—we realize that the church, as conceived by Metochites, was even more cluttered than today and that its opulence must have been quite bewildering.

What is, however, more significant about Kahriye Camii and, in fact, all other Palaeologan churches is that the relation between architecture and decoration has broken down. Each picture has become an entity in its own right, and it is as big or as small as the space available for it: hence disregard for scale. The rediscovery of picture space was, of course, the major disruptive element, and its application in Kahriye Camii is of considerable interest.

In the narrative scenes the action takes place on a kind of stage which is delimited by a backdrop. The elements of the backdrop are of antique inspiration, but they are disposed in a manner that cannot fail to confuse us: for the perspective is based not on one, but on several simultaneous points of view. The vault composition combining the Fondling of the infant Virgin by her parents and her Presentation to the high priests may serve to illustrate the principles involved. In the former scene we have a common type of backdrop consisting of a wall with two projecting pavilions. Now, whereas the structure on the right as well as the bench on which the family is seated are seen from above, the structure on the left is seen from below. In the Presentation scene the three priests are meant to be seated within a concave exedra, but instead of curving in, the exedra curves out. The projection of this structure is from a worm's eye view, yet the table in front of the priests tips forward as if it were seen from above, and the bench on which the right-hand priest sits is viewed from an even steeper height so that it seems to be falling over.

Such disconcerting experimentation with perspective is susceptible to various interpretations, but it shows, at any rate, a deep and as yet uncomprehending preoccupation with the third dimension. The effect achieved is one of fairyland unreality. The fantastic settings are populated with small-headed, elongated figures which have a tendency to walk on tiptoe and are wrapped in voluminous garments that seem to be somehow inflated from within. The style of these works is anything but monumental —rather we are made to think of enlarged miniatures—and basically unsuitable for the medium of mosaic.

In the frescoes of the funeral chapel the artists were evidently more at home, and here they produced the one indubitable masterpiece of Kahriye Camii, the Anastasis (Harrowing of Hell). Crowded though it may be by "classical" Byzantine standards, the composition has a powerful triangular structure. The luminous figure of Christ —all whites and opalescent greys—strides energetically in the bleak setting of the underworld. Pulled up by his firm grip, the inert figures of Adam and Eve float out of their tombs. Indeed, all of the energy is concentrated in Christ: the two balanced groups of the righteous cluster round as passive spectators, some of them not so much standing as suspended, ghost-like, in the air. Passive and exhausted, the Byzantine Empire, too, was pinning all its hopes on the advent of Christ, the only force capable of resuscitating it.

Palaeologan painting was the last creative manifestation of Byzantine art. It has often been called a renaissance, yet its antiquarian elements appear to have been due not so much to a direct and invigorating contact with classical remains, as to rummaging among old manuscripts. Less vigorous than the Italian Duecento and Trecento, more tradition-bound, Palaeologan painting grappled nevertheless with the same basic problem, that of pictorial space. Had conditions been favorable, it might have developed in the same direction as Italian art, but the death of Byzantium prevented this from happening. Progressively fossilized, Palaeologan painting remained the artistic idiom of the subjugated Greeks until the early nineteenth century. A hundred years before Constantinople fell, however, the last Byzantine artist of genius, Theophanes the Greek, carried Palaeologan painting to Russia and there, transformed by a different artistic intuition, it produced works of unrivalled beauty.

THE ISLAMIC PERIOD

ANKARA, ARSLAN HANE MOSQUE. MIHRAB (PRAYER NICHE) COMPOSED OF FAIENCE MOSAIC AND STUCCOWORK. ABOUT 1289.

THE SELJUK, MONGOL, AND EMIRATE DYNASTIES

THE splendor of the skyline of Istanbul and the rich variety of Turkish objects in our museums have prompted a widespread belief that "Turkish art" is synonymous with the art of the Ottoman Sultans. This, however, is not the case. Indeed, the history of the Turks in Anatolia started 255 years before the Ottomans conquered Bursa (known in the West as Brussa) in 1326 and made it their first major capital. Even this initial appearance of Turks in Anatolia in the last third of the eleventh century is not the beginning of Turkish history and of the manifestations of Turkish elements in the art of the Near and Middle East. Already in the middle of the sixth century there existed in Central Asia—that is, in Turkestan, or "the land of the Turks"—two very large Turkish empires about which we are informed by contemporary Chinese historians. The northern kingdom was destroyed by another Turkish group, the Uigurs, who ruled over this territory from 745 until 854, although a small principality continued to exist in Kan-su, China, until the middle of the thirteenth century. Buddhism spread amongst these Turks in the beginning of the seventh century, but in 762 they made Manichaeanism their state religion. By contrast, Islam made inroads rather late. However, Turks also played a role in the Near East and then as Muslims, although at first not as a close and organized group. They had been imported from Central Asia in large numbers as slaves who were famous for their physical beauty and military prowess. In that capacity, they served in Near Eastern courts as pages and soldiers and became particularly important as the bodyguards of the Abbasid caliphs in Baghdad in the ninth century. These Turkish soldiers were so ubiquitous and played such an important role that an Arab poet of the period expressed the fear that one day they would drive the Arabs back to their deserts. High government officials, too, were selected from this military contingent. One of these was Ahmed the son of Tulun who first became Governor of Egypt in 868 and then established himself as semi-independent ruler of that country and founder of a dynasty which ruled until 906. The Tulunids were later on followed by another Turkish dynasty, the Ikhshidids (from 935 to 969).

Turkish rulers were of even greater importance in areas close to Central Asia. Thus, a Turkish dynasty, the Ghaznevids, after having brought down one of the most brilliant Iranian kingdoms, created a large kingdom of their own which included Eastern Iran, the regions which are now Afghanistan, and Northern India (962 to 1191). The rule of this family was followed by another Turkish dynasty, the Ghorids, who built as their new capital the city of Firozkoh in Central Afghanistan, the main remnant of which, a very tall, beautifully decorated minaret built between 1163 and 1202, has only recently been discovered. Indeed, rulers of Turkish extraction were to appear for hundreds of years throughout the Near and Middle East and well beyond what is usually conceived of as Turkish territory. We mention only the Mamluk Sultans of Egypt who ruled over the country of the Nile for over 250 years and who commissioned great and dazzling works of art and architecture (1250 to 1517); the Sultans of the White and Black Turkomans who were masters over great parts of Iran in the fifteenth century; the Safavid Shahs of Iran who, from the beginning of the sixteenth century, stimulated one of the most lavish and luxurious epochs in architecture, painting, and the decorative arts which the world has ever seen; and finally the Mughal Emperors of India (1526 to 1858) who in their heyday were the overlords of a vast subcontinent and reigned in fabulous courts.

From the point of view of Turkish history, the most important role played by any Turkish people in Near Eastern history prior to the appearance of the Turks in Asia Minor is, however, that of the Seljuks who, as members of the Central-Asian Ghuzz or Oghuz tribal group, had invaded Iran in 1038 and had made themselves so powerful that the Abbasid caliphs in Baghdad appointed them "Kings of the East and West." Four outstanding rulers usually referred to as the "Great Seljuks" instigated what is undoubtedly one of the most sophisticated and sumptuous arts of Iran in the Middle Ages. The central government of the Great Seljuks came to an end in 1157 and disintegrated into many semi-independent principalities in Iraq, Mesopotamia, and Syria, each of which fostered architecture and the decorative arts to a high degree.

It was in the Seljuk period that an old dream of the Islamic world finally came true and was realized in at least its first stage. In the formative years of early Islam when the armies of the new religion carved out an empire that eventually reached from Spain to India, the only region which withstood the repeated onslaughts by land and sea was the heartland of the Byzantine Empire, composed of Anatolia and the area around its great capital city, Constantinople. In the centuries succeeding this early period, a limited, periodic border war had existed along the eastern and southern frontiers of Anatolia. There were continuous raids; and at times one side or the other was able to push the frontier further into enemy territory, though on the whole the dividing line was stable. However, the second Great Seljuk, Alp Arslan, succeeded in defeating the Byzantine Emperor Romanus IV Diogenes near Manzikert (Malazgirt), north of Lake Van, in 1071 and in taking him prisoner. The illustrious captive was soon freed again, and peace was made since the Sultan did not think of furthering his victory under the specific political conditions. However, this defeat opened up the country to large-scale raids and warfare; and before long the whole region was conquered by the Muslim *ghazis*, or "warriors of the faith." A member of the Seljuk family, Suleyman, son of Qutulmish, then became head of the Muslim forces; he selected Nicaea as his residence in 1081 which was renamed Iznik. But this symbolic choice of a town so close to the capital of the Byzantine Empire was premature. A few years later, in 1097, Nicaea was retaken by the Byzantine forces with the support of the Crusaders and the western part of Anatolia, too, was lost.

The entire first half of the twelfth century was politically and culturally an unsettled period which saw not only fighting between Muslims and Byzantines but also a strong rivalry in the Muslim camp between the Seljuk and the Danishmand families and with the princes in East and Southeast Anatolia. Eventually, however, the Seljuks were able to settle down in the plains of Iconium where they established a capital which they renamed Konya. In 1176 they managed to defeat the Byzantines once more in an important battle in the Pass of Chardak (Myriokephaloi) which prevented further attacks of the Byzantine army and led to a stabilizing of the Byzantine-Muslim frontier. Towards the end of the twelfth century, the Muslim state was well enough organized politically and secure enough financially to allow extensive cultural activities, particularly in the fields of architecture and the decorative arts. The very end of that century and, in particular, the first half of the thirteenth century represent the flowering of the Seljuk State from which great monuments have survived since most of them were solidly built of stone. In 1243 the Mongols, who had inflicted such tremendous havoc on the eastern parts of the Muslim world, defeated the Seljuk Sultan at Közedağ. The Seljuk rulers were still able to retain their thrones, though under strict Mongol supervision eventually exercised by a special Mongol functionary. Even in the final decades of Seljuk rule from which coins with royal names were issued till 1302, fine monuments and objects continued to be created. These demonstrate the persistence of the momentum gathered in the first half of the thirteenth century, by virtue of which the arts flourished unabated and often took on more florid forms.

However, though the Seljuks constituted the leading dynasty, they were not the only rulers of Anatolia. In the twelfth century there were the rival dynasties of the Danish-mands in Sivas and Malatya, the Salduqids in Erzurum, the Banu Mengüjeks in Erzincan and Divriği, and still other emirs ruling temporarily as semi-independent princes, some to become Seljuk vassals in the thirteenth century while others were to disappear altogether. Furthermore, it must not be forgotten that the southeastern area of Anatolia had had a very much longer period of Muslim history than the central and eastern regions. This section had been conquered by Muslim armies around 640 and was thus included in the part of the Caliphate called the Jazira (i.e. "Island" or "Peninsula"), that is the northern part of the land between the Euphrates and the

Tigris. Typical for the region is the town of Diyarbakır (or Amid) on the Tigris which, after a long period of Umayyad and Abbasid administration, became in 990 the capital of the Kurdish Marwanids, to be ruled later on by the Great Seljuks, then by the Turkish Inalids; these in turn fell under the sway of the Nisanids, whose reign was finally superseded by the Artuqids coming from earlier capitals in Hisn-Kaifa (now Hasankeyf), Kharput and Mardin. Similarly checkered histories, at times interspersed with Byzantine dominion, were the lot of such well-known towns as Malatya, Silvan (formerly Mayyafariqin), Urfa (formerly ar-Ruha, and still earlier Edessa), Harran, Mardin, Nusaybin (formerly Nasibin, Nisibis), and others, all of which played an important part clearly reflected in their monuments.

With the weakening of the central power of the Seljuk Sultans toward the end of the thirteenth century, the various parts of Anatolia strove for independence. As a result, the country became divided into ten emirates or principalities; that of the Karamans in the Konya region was at first the most important. Since many uprooted and dispossessed persons and also heretics—among them many fervent, even fanatic, believers from Central Asia—had fled to Anatolia on account of the savage Mongol conquests, a new ghazi spirit was kindled, especially in the principality of Osman in the northwest, whose ruler proudly called himself: "Sultan, son of the Sultan of the Ghazis, Ghazi, son of Ghazi, marquis of the horizons, hero of the world." The Byzantine frontier, here quite close to the imperial capital, was increasingly under attack from this source; and, since the Greeks had weakened their Anatolian front line by transferring troops to the Balkans, this second Turkish invasion finally broke down the enemy's resistance. By 1340 nearly the whole of northwestern Anatolia had been taken by the Ottomans including the important towns of Bursa and Nicaea which fell in 1326 and 1331 respectively. From this at first rather modest base, the Ottomans then set out to create an empire which has left us a unique art and civilization.

In speaking of these past political events, the people themselves should not be forgotten as they represent the actors in these happenings. It seems therefore proper to quote what is certainly an unbiased report from the end of the period we are discussing. In it the highly educated Moroccan traveler Ibn Battuta who in 1333 had visited Anatolia summarizes his impressions in the following words (in H.A.R. Gibb's translation): "This country called *Bilad al-Rum* (i.e. the land of the Rhomaeans or Byzantines) is one of the finest regions in the world; in it God has brought together the good things dispersed through other lands. Its inhabitants are the comeliest of men in form, the cleanest in dress, the most delicious in food, and the kindliest of God's creatures. This is why the saying goes 'Blessing in Syria and kindliness in al-Rum.' Wherever we stopped in this land, whether at hospice or private house, our neighbours both men and women (who do not veil themselves) came to ask after our needs . . . Their men used to bring us warm bread on the day it was baked, together with delicious viands to go with it, as a special treat for us, and would say to us 'The women have sent this

DIVRIĞI, GREAT MOSQUE. DETAIL OF NORTH PORTAL. 1228.

to you and beg of you a prayer.' . . . When we left them to continue our journey, they bade us farewell as though they were our relatives and our own kin, and you would see the women weeping out of grief at our departure."

To this comment a statement by the historian Ibn Bibi about one of the outstanding rulers of the time might be added. In it he says that the Sultan Ala eddin Kay-Kobad (1220-1237) "showed immense ability in architecture and various crafts, such as the forging of knives, the making of sculpture, paintings and saddlery, and that he was a connoisseur of jewels as well." Even if one assumes that we are here confronted with a case of poetical and courtly license, a remark of this nature reflects at least a strong active interest in the arts.

The artistic flowering in *Rum* or Anatolia in the thirteenth century represents one of the most spectacular developments of the Islamic world in the Middle Ages, especially since the basic conditions were seemingly none too propitious. The ruling dynasty in Konya was only a collateral branch of the great Seljuk family, and its domain was to a large extent a mountainous region with a severe climate. The country had been conquered only slightly more than 100 to 150 years before by rough "warriors of the faith" and Turkoman tribes who not many generations previously had roamed the steppes of Central Asia. These basic groups had since been joined by Byzantine and Armenian converts, fugitives from the Mongols from the eastern parts of the Muslim world, and an influx of merchants, artisans, sheykhs, and dervishes. There would hardly appear to have been time for these heterogeneous elements to amalgamate and produce an integrated art of their own. But in spite of natural handicaps, an initial development full of turmoil, and the different and equally variegated history of the southeastern area, the many towns of the whole region became artistic nuclei in which the various rulers as the main patrons successfully produced outstanding buildings and objects. The individual style of these works usually sets them clearly apart from the artistic achievements in the rest of the Muslim world and we are at the same time surprised by their versatility, wealth of imagination, and ingenuity in finding new ways of formal expression. Altogether the art of Anatolia in the thirteenth century is as miraculous a phenomenon as the sudden conquest of the country in the late eleventh.

The largest and most important buildings within the towns were the mosques, particularly the chief mosques used for the Friday service. As everywhere in the Muslim world, one of the traditional prototypes followed was the Arab hypostyle mosque. Here, in a broad, shallow building, a series of rows of columns or pillars support the roof of the main sanctuary which is located on one side of a large courtyard surrounded by porticoes; this is the system, for instance, of the Great Mosque in Sivas which may possibly date from the Danishmand period. In other, architecturally more ambitious buildings, the central nave leading to the *mihrab* or prayer niche is wider and often contains a large dome in front of the niche or a whole series of such domes between niche and entrance door. Although there are certain irregularities in the general layout, possibly due to the topographical situation, and several building periods, this is the scheme found in the best known of the ancient mosques of the country, that of Ala eddin in Konya. Here as in other mosques and buildings the supports are from pre-Islamic monuments, particularly churches; this not only means a convenient re-use of ancient, cut material but also implies symbolically the victory of the new faith over the old. Both the simple hypostyle mosque and its enriched version with a specially stressed, central nave and *mihrab* area have prototypes in Iraq, Syria, Egypt, and North Africa. On the other hand, there does not seem to have been an extensive use of the newly developed, Persian-type mosque which places in the middle of each of the four sides of the courtyard a high, recessed, vaulted hall, the *eyvan*, followed on the sanctuary side by a large dome before the *mihrab*. Nor are the domes always placed on squinches—that is, on arches thrown across the corners of the square chamber below after the manner of the Iranian architects; instead the dome is often supported by triangular pendentives in the four corners or by a whole frieze-like series of triangular units of alternating directions which form the transition zone.

The disinclination to take over important architectural schemes employed by the Great Seljuks indicates clearly that Anatolian art in this century must not be regarded as a mere provincial version of the Seljuk art of Iran. Actually, unlike their colleagues in Iran, some of the Anatolian architects were more true to their Turkish traditions; for instance, in a number of mosques they employed wooden columns the use of which had been customary in Turkestan in the tenth to the twelfth centuries and was then possibly inspired by the wooden tent pole of the nomadic tent. But apart from following these earlier traditions in the Islamic world, the Seljuk architects also went their own way and used resources peculiar to their new country, thus developing a new type of mosque not found anywhere else. In it the sanctuary approaches the aspect of a basilica by having a longitudinal orientation and a central nave that is wider than the side aisles; there is also no longer the traditional forecourt, though it could be said that the courtyard is now placed within the building, as there is, at times, an open area in the middle of the central nave. Since the high ceilings of these buildings, as we find them in the Great Mosque in Divriği or in the Burmalı Minare and Gök Medrese Mosques in Amasya, are also variously and skillfully vaulted, these interiors give the impression of a Western-medieval ecclesiastical building. This is in no way astonishing since the origin of this type of architecture is to be looked for in Byzantine churches which the architects of the thirteenth century, like the Muslim builders of the late seventh and eighth centuries, had no compunction against using for their own purposes. In following these Western models, the Turkish rulers and their architects initiated a trend which continued to characterize a good deal of Turkish art throughout the following centuries. However, it is significant that the adoption of a basilica-like scheme was not slavishly pursued, as the omission of the narthex, which had no liturgical or ceremonial significance in a mosque, clearly indicates.

DIVRIĞI, GREAT MOSQUE. NORTH PORTAL. 1228.

A confrontation of three remarkable sculptured portals presents us with the wide range of Seljuk decorative elements and their surprisingly different compositions and acquaints us as well with the difficulties of interpretation. Thus the more restrained, better integrated and basically two-dimensional Portal of the Medrese of Karatay of Konya would seem to be the earliest building of the series; yet it belongs in the year 1251/1252 and is thus probably the second. But it was inspired by the gateway of the Sultan Ala eddin Mosque in Konya, dated 1220/1221; furthermore, its Damascene architect, Muhammad b. Khawlan, has apparently transplanted into Anatolia the earlier, sober architecture of Syria, and in particular its angularly knotted ribbons and the two staggered rows of half-circles crossing each other which occur in both mosque and medrese. The undated doorway of the Ince Minare Medrese in Konya might well have seemed to stand second in our group on account of its contrasting two-dimensional decorations and the stressing of sculptural elements; but in 1258 the same architect, Kaluk b. Abdullah, erected another stylistically related building, the Mosque of Sahib Ata, and it is therefore quite likely that this portal is chronologically the last of the three. The strangest case of all is the North Gate of the Mosque of Divriği. This seems the most baroque, disjointed and strangely three-dimensional in general treatment and in the character of its details. But it dates from 1228/1229 and is therefore the first of the series. One can only surmise that the architect Khurramshah of Ahlat (in Eastern Anatolia) who worked for the Mengüjekid Ahmed Shah was still groping for the right approach to architectural stone carving for which he applied principles of stucco and metalwork without, however, fully finding the right morphological setting.

KONYA, INCE MINARE MEDRESE. PORTAL. THIRD QUARTER OF THE 13TH CENTURY.

KONYA, KARATAY MEDRESE. PORTAL. 1251.

SIVAS, GÖK (OR BLUE) MEDRESE. FAÇADE. 1271.

In 1271/1272 three splendidly decorated medreses were built in Sivas—one of them by an Iranian from Barujird—which attests to the thriving Seljuk economy. The best preserved among these, the Gök (or "Blue") Medrese by Master Kaluyan of Konya follows the traditional four-eyvaned scheme, enriched by a portico on its long sides and turquoise and purple faience decorations on its minarets, in its oratory and interior eyvans. What distinguishes this building (and its two mates) from earlier structures is the fact that it contains more than a tall sculptured portal in an otherwise bare or unevenly treated wall, but presents an integrated façade in which all parts form an ensemble. Its reputation is apparent from the description by the seventeenth-century Turkish traveler Evliya Chelebi: "When Timur saw it, he bit his finger in astonishment... It had as high a portal as a fortress... On its façade the master carved all the flowers created by God in such a manner that everybody... believes himself before a work of magic... Formerly the gifts to this school were so bountiful that every day one could supply the students eight services of excellent food placed on Chinese porcelain..."

While Iranian prototypes were only rarely used for mosque structures, they were closely followed for the *medreses* or religious seminaries; here, in the larger buildings, four central *eyvans* and intermediary cells for students were deployed around an open courtyard; to this scheme two domed funerary chambers at the side of the rear *eyvan* were usually added. In some of the smaller buildings the architect was satisfied with two *eyvans*, one serving as entrance hall and the second as the main place of assembly on the opposite side of the courtyard, the cells for the students being, as usual, placed on the lateral confines. More important for the further development was the novel idea of placing a dome over what in other buildings had been an open court. In this way the Anatolian architects achieved a centrally composed, domed building, thereby creating an architectural prototype which prefigured the large, domed structures of Constantinople and the other main cities of the Turkish empire.

The decoration of the buildings centered on the *mihrabs* and even more so around the façade, particularly the often projecting, monumental main entrance gates whose height usually surpasses that of the lateral walls. The doors are placed in a recess and topped by a tall half-dome composed of many corbelling units called *muqarnas* in the Arabic lingua franca of the Near East (and incorrectly rendered as stalactite vaults in the West). This basic unit is then in turn surrounded by a very dense and complex, decorative ensemble which consists of bands with geometric or arabesque patterns as well as epigraphic panels; at times there are spectacular, large-scale leaf designs in high relief and occasionally even animal motifs, the latter being an unheard-of feature in the sacred architecture of Islam. The kaleidoscopically sparkling combination of motifs and their hypnotic fascination reflects an aesthetic approach far removed from Mediterranean reason and restraint. Large-scale patterns may alternate with small ones. Flat designs are suddenly interrupted by elements in high relief. Units turn, loop, or twist; or they are combined in a manner which defies logical anticipation. Thus, a thin, engaged column may support a very thick, stubby one which is in turn topped by a tall, spiral variety and finally by another covered with an imbricate pattern; or columns suddenly turn to the side at sharp right angles as if they were made not of stone but of metal pipes. Then again they show large superimposed floral patterns which apply accents and create at the same time a sense of affluence. Even when rather restrained, the designs are astounding in their variety and the boldness with which elements of different nature are juxtaposed. The motifs in high relief are undoubtedly inspired by Persian stuccowork, as the stippled surface patterns indicate, while individual elements may hail from other regions, such as the braided or interlocking bands which were a favorite Syrian motif, the cushioned voussoirs occurring first in Fatimid Egypt, and the notched joints in the wedge-shaped stones forming arches commonly found in many Western-Mediterranean buildings. It would be false to deride this decoration as overdone, exaggeratedly Baroque, or even as barbaric. Since in theological and mystical thinking the gate has a profound meaning as a mysterious passageway leading from everyday being to a heightened existence, this type of decoration with its intense vitality was apparently meant to elevate this part of the structure, and thereby the building itself, into something out of the ordinary; and, as (in contrast to Iranian decoration) the given elements are never alluring to the senses, they imply a different, grander world beyond everyday human emotions. In the case of those gates where fantastic floral patterns of large size abound (as in Divriği), one might also assume that here, just as in early Islamic (and early Christian) shrines, the architect implied the concept of the paradise garden. That there is a definite iconographic intention is quite clear from the unorthodox use of animal designs. Here, the precise meaning still often escapes us; in certain instances the animals appear to be like coats of arms possibly based on ancient totemistic beliefs. In others some old mythological legends seem to linger on, such as a struggle between a snake or dragon from the nether world and a celestial bird; again there may be some underlying cosmological or astrological concept; or the aim may be merely apotropaic and magic in a general way. Whatever the interpretation, in this respect also the Anatolian princes and their architects have gone novel ways.

The architects not only created the decorations around the gateways but they further accented the rounded corners forming engaged, half-size towers which represented the lateral confines of the building. This stressing of the main parts of the façade —the all-important, projecting central entrance gate, the corner towers, and secondary elements in between such as windows or fountain recesses—all these are features which had already occurred in the Arab world, initially in Tunisia and in a more developed fashion in Egypt; but here their rendition surpasses anything created in the Mediterranean sphere. Novel too, at least in the manner in which they are introduced, are certain other features in the building. Thus we find here for the first time the frequent use of a pair of circular brick minarets rising right and left above the entrance gate and ending in a pointed tip just above the projecting balcony for the muezzin. This combination proved to be so successful that it appears constantly in the Persian mosques, *medreses*, and gateways of the fourteenth and later centuries. Syrian architecture of the Turkish Zengid rulers had already combined the mausolea with the *medrese*; but this was now done in an outwardly more spectacular fashion and also in a manner which is architecturally more suitable, as in Erzurum, where the mausoleum is placed along the main axis of the building beyond the *eyvan* opposite the entrance gate.

While the interior stone carvings on framing mouldings, capitals, and *mihrabs* are rather restrained when compared with the more spectacular displays around the entrance gates, the architect nevertheless had at his command other means of creating dramatic effects. The most impressive of these and certainly the most colorful are the mosaics of specially shaped turquoise and purple, at times also white and dark blue, bits of tile with which the dadoes of the side walls, the framing arches, the walls of the *eyvans*, the domes and their pendentives, and particularly the *mihrabs* of some mosques and *medreses* were decorated. For nearly a hundred and fifty years Iranian builders

KONYA, KARATAY MEDRESE. INTERIOR WITH FAIENCE MOSAIC DECORATION. 1251.

SULTAN HAN NEAR AKSARAY. HALL. 1229.

had experimented with the creation of colorful design by means of specially cut, glazed and unglazed ceramic units combined to form specific patterns. One can follow the development of this technique step by step from its humble beginnings in the first part of the twelfth century; but while in Iran, as far as we can see, it never arrived at the stage of total coverage of the wall surfaces before the beginning of the fourteenth century, this stage was reached in Anatolia possibly as early as 1220 (in the *mihrab* of the Ala eddin Mosque) and certainly by 1242. It then appeared in a manner which was technically perfect although the designs were subsequently made more complex by more minute and elaborate patterns executed in a larger range of colors. But while these later examples, especially in Iran, revealed an unheard-of skill and ornamental sophistication, the Anatolian examples of geometric and epigraphic decorations dating from the middle and second half of the thirteenth century have never been surpassed in their monumental dignity. It is true that the faience mosaic in one of the earliest buildings with this decorative technique, that is the Sırçalı Medrese in Konya of 1242, was signed by one Muhammad, son of Muhammad, son of Othman, builder from Tus (in Eastern Iran). However, it is not the origin of this artisan—possibly an Iranian refugee uprooted by the Mongol invasion—that is as significant as the second part of the inscription, which states: "I have made this decoration the like of which occurs nowhere else in the world. I do not last, but it remains, a memento of myself."

Quite clearly an artist was, in this dynamic milieu, for the first time given the chance to pursue the ultimate possibilities of this type of decoration and thus achieve something never done before. One ceramic artist in the late Seljuk period (about 1289) explored still another effect of this technique by combining in a *mihrab* a brilliantly colored but flat faience mosaic with a monochrome and mat stucco decoration executed as a high, deeply carved relief and also by juxtaposing in the two media geometric and epigraphic patterns with floral designs. This type of surface decoration far exceeds the earlier, timid experiments of a similar kind in Iran and even those of the East Anatolian border region; yet it is nevertheless found in a simple mosque built in the traditionally Turkish manner with wooden columns, the Arslan Hane Mosque of Ankara, then a town of secondary importance. Judging from these artistic creations, one can well gauge the dynamic and inventive surge which must have swept through the whole country.

While the mosques and the *medreses* represent the major category of large buildings in the towns, the most ubiquitous, smaller structures are the *türbes* or mausolea. The great majority of these have a round or octagonal shape over a square base and are topped by a conical roof which covers an upper chamber containing the cenotaph; the actual tomb is located in a crypt below. These buildings may stand by themselves in the towns or in the country although they are sometimes built in connection with religious structures and can even have their own specifically designed enclosures. Like all the other major buildings, these monuments are executed in stone; they show arcading on the outside wall which may be further decorated with geometric, floral, and even animal designs; the same designs are also to be found just below the roof. The shape of these buildings seems to go back ultimately to that of the ancient nomadic tent. There are related structures in Soviet Azerbaijan, and even closer connections exist with East-Christian structures of a similar nature. The one major exception is the shrine of the celebrated mystic poet Jelal eddin Rumi who lived and died in Konya (in 1273); but even here a round tower with a cone-shaped roof covers the resting place of the revered saint, though the blue-glazed cylindrical tower has a polylobed outline in its cross-section. Next to this mausoleum is the later Ottoman *tekke* or monastery of the Order of the Mevlevis (known in the West as the "Whirling Dervishes") which after Rumi had established it spread to other parts of the country, especially Constantinople; however, such monasteries existed already in the thirteenth century as the historian Ibn Bibi spoke of them in his account of that period.

ANKARA, ALA EDDIN MOSQUE. CARVED WOODEN MIMBER (PULPIT). 1197-1198.

Another significant group of medieval buildings, which clearly reveal a sense of social responsibility on the part of their founders, is that of the hospitals, of which four, all of them large, have come down to us: in Kayseri (1205), Sivas (1217), Divriği (1228), and one somewhat later from the Mongol period in Amasya (1308). They follow the *medrese* scheme although examination rooms and wards appropriate to their purpose are now included. Their close proximity to either a mosque or a *medrese* indicates that the motivation for this type of building was religious. They were built by royal command and in the case of Sivas the king was even buried inside. Indicative of the personal involvement of royal ladies in these charities is the fact that in two instances the inscriptions mention the buildings to be either a gift of, or a bequest by, a princess, while in a third case the name of the royal consort is at least mentioned together with that of the sultan. The finest example is the hospital in Divriği, which is built wall-to-wall with the mosque and in the same beautiful yellow stone. The elaborately decorated portal as well as the more restrained stone carvings of its very monumental interior make it outstanding among all the buildings of the period.

There exists one additional large type of Seljuk building in Central Anatolia which, though numerous as well as impressive in appearance, is only rarely seen by present-day travelers because the surviving examples are found along the old medieval roads which radiated from Konya and Kayseri, they being then the most important Anatolian cities; and these highways are in most cases no longer used today. These are the old *hans* or caravanserais spaced usually about 20 to 25 miles from each other. Fifty-eight of these are fairly well preserved; thirty-nine others may include some which also belong to the Seljuk period, but their ruined state no longer permits a definite attribution. By comparison, there exist only one or two such structures of the same period, built of brick, in Iran and seven in Syria—for which, as in Anatolia, the more durable stone was used. Five caravanserais follow the Persian and Syrian scheme of having a number of open or closed rooms along the four sides of a large square courtyard which is accessible by a single gate and protected by high walls with a sequence of massive towers along the circumference. The fully evolved "Anatolian" type consists, however, of a more elaborate combination not found elsewhere in the Muslim world. This adds to the court ensemble with rooms on three sides a large, more solidly built, longitudinal hall which has a high central nave and a sequence of from five to nine lower aisles running at right angles to the central axis; the second unit was regarded as the most important part of the caravanserai and was also the first to be built. The ceilings are constructed as tunnel vaults, and the very center of the central nave is furthermore crowned with a dome on a high drum. The general effect of these central, high-vaulted halls—the largest measures 15,386 square feet and is thus only slightly smaller than the nave of Mainz Cathedral—is much like that of a western medieval church; and this impression is voiced by all the earlier travelers and writers on the subject. Yet as the troughs in the aisles indicate, these structures were primarily used as stables, though they may have also served as storerooms and night-quarters for the travelers. Their main decoration is found on the single, projecting portal through which the traveler entered the courtyard and on the second portal on the main axis which leads into the stable hall. The most spectacular of these structures are the so-called Sultan Hans of which the earliest dates from 1229 though the type seems to have existed around 1190. Altogether the dates actually given or construable indicate a main building span between 1205 and 1278 with the most active period between 1229 and 1250. At least nine *hans* were erected by the sultans themselves; five are due to a queen —Mahperi Hatun—while others were provided by high dignitaries and even private persons. They reveal an unusual awareness of the basic significance of the caravan trade and of the importance of such protective hostels in a wild country. It seems again symptomatic of this civilization that it provided a novel and unusual solution of the problem and that the resulting buildings are remarkable both for their true functionalism and high architectural quality.

This list of buildings does not yet exhaust the architectural program of the Seljuks. To name only a few other types: There are large fortifications designed to protect citadels on hillsides outside of towns and others for the towns themselves. Then there are the palaces and pavilions of the rulers, built both in the towns and at the beautiful sites in the country, one of them, at Kubadabad, even designed by the Sultan himself, with all its domes, colored walls and paintings. Another important group of buildings of which we know mainly from the sources are those dedicated to the common weal, such as hospices for the sheltering of travelers in towns, houses for the use of religious and secular fraternities, bazaars, and bathhouses. Finally there are the gracefully curved bridges on massive arches, some of them still in use today.

The rather simple service in the mosque, unlike that of the church, did not necessitate a considerable amount of furniture and elaborate objects. However, the few that were needed formed a definite challenge to the artisans; thus, each of the major mosques in which the Friday service was conducted needed a *mimber* or pulpit which in that period was always constructed of wood. It consists basically of about a dozen steps which are entered by an ornamental door and lead up to a platform covered by a pyramidal canopy. On each side of the stairs is a large, triangular panel combined with a rectangular field below the platform area. Finally there is a railing on either side of the staircase which is usually rendered as openwork carpentry. A complex, all-over, geometric configuration covers the sides of the *mimber* and forms the skeleton for the many, irregularly shaped inserts filled with elaborate arabesques carved in relief on more than one level; calligraphically rendered inscription panels give the name of the donor, usually the sultan himself, and also those of the carver and date. Possibly the oldest is the one in the Ala eddin Mosque in Konya which dates from 1155.

The wood carvers also created the decorations on doors, window shutters, cenotaphs, railings, and, to judge from at least one surviving later example, on *mihrabs*. This prayer niche comes from the village of Damse Köy to the southwest of Ürgüp which, just prior to 1350, was the residence of a prince. Its dense but sober and well-integrated decoration combines geometric and epigraphic panels and to a lesser degree adds arabesque designs, especially for framing borders. It is an unusually impressive piece, which shows that even in the period following the Seljuk period the high quality of craftsmanship did not decline. This wooden *mihrab* had Seljuk precursors in twelfth-century Syria; but here again the Anatolian craftsman has used the inspiration from abroad for a different and specifically Anatolian creation.

CARVED WOODEN MIHRAB (PRAYER NICHE) FROM THE MOSQUE OF DAMSE KÖY. FIRST HALF OF THE 14TH CENTURY.
ETHNOGRAPHIC MUSEUM, ANKARA.

BRONZE KANDIL (LAMPSHADE) FOR A MOSQUE, MADE IN KONYA BY ALI, SON OF MUHAMMAD OF NISIBIS. 1280.
ETHNOGRAPHIC MUSEUM, ANKARA.

Another typically Islamic wooden utensil popular in Seljuk Anatolia is the *rahle* or
folding reading stand, primarily used for Korans, of which the finest was made in 1279
for the mausoleum of Jelal eddin Rumi in Konya. Its outside panels are densely carved
with richly modulated Seljuk arabesques which were originally gilded, accentuated in
red, and set against a dark green background. Although the basic motifs are the same
throughout, the carver understood the need for varying them. Thus, the arabesques
in the border of the upper part appear as bands, thereby forming a contrast to the wide,
symmetrical arrangements in the center panels; then there are the arabesques set

RAHLE (KORAN READING STAND) OF CARVED AND PAINTED WOOD,
MADE FOR THE MAUSOLEUM (TÜRBE) OF JELAL EDDIN RUMI IN KONYA. 1279. KONYA MUSEUM.

within spiral scrolls in the spandrels of the lower part which show greater movement than the more sculpturally treated, central, flower-like composition. In addition, there are some variations in spacing and surface treatment. While there are other *rahles* with spirited arabesque designs and inscriptions in *nashki* writing, this Koran stand is unique in having on its inside panels a design in tempera painting under a golden-yellow varnish. A roundel in the central section contains a heraldically rendered, double-headed bird set against a background of spiral scrolls from which arabesques and fourteen lions emanate. All this is painted in gold outlined with black on a red background, while the golden floral motifs in the four corner spandrels are placed on a light blue ground that now appears green. It is remarkable that an animal decoration such as this should occur on an object which is so closely connected with sacred readings in a shrine; but, as we have already seen, the Rum Seljuks showed a special predilection for figural representations even in a religious context. Both types of animals found on this *rahle* are emblems of royal power and in all probability go back to totemistic beliefs. They occur in this combination also on one of the towers of the important town of Diyarbakır. What is, however, of special interest here is the additional fact that the design is executed in the same technique as that used for Byzantine icons; being a unique specimen, we do not know whether there were possibly others which are now lost or whether this represents a rare Muslim offshoot from the Greek tradition executed with a purely Seljuk theme.

The *rahle* naturally presupposes the existence of Koran manuscripts, calligraphically written and illuminated in Anatolia and particularly in its capital, Konya. There are at least two such volumes known, although others undoubtedly exist and have merely not yet been found and published. One was written (on paper—as were all the manuscripts of that date and of course later ones as well) by Kutluğ, son of Abdullah, in 1238 and decorated in a limited fashion (now in the Shrine of Jelal eddin Rumi). The other, though of small size, is richly illuminated with many differently conceived ornamental pages; this is a manuscript of 1278 written in Konya itself by the Konya scribe al-Hasan, son of Juban, son of Abdullah (now in the Chester Beatty Library, Dublin). The shrine of Jelal eddin Rumi contains, furthermore, a whole series of beautifully illuminated manuscripts of the works of the great mystic, especially copies of his major work, the *Methnevi*, and those of his son, Sultan Veled. The earliest is of the year 1278 while others are from various dates in the fourteenth century when the gold configurations on red burnished gold or lapis-lazuli blue backgrounds become more and more spectacular and complex in composition. This development demonstrates again how the momentum achieved in the Seljuk period continued without letup in the subsequent Mongol and Emirate periods.

Another unique object which once formed part of the furnishings of the Eşref Süleyman Mosque in Beyşehir is a bronze *kandil* or lamp, originally gilt, made in Konya in 1280 by Ali, son of Muhammad, of Nisibis, a town on the Turkish-Syrian border,

KNOTTED CARPET FROM THE ALA EDDIN MOSQUE IN KONYA. CENTRAL ANATOLIA, 13TH CENTURY.
MUSEUM OF TURKISH AND ISLAMIC ART, ISTANBUL.

LEAD BIRD FORMING THE SPOUT OF A FOUNTAIN. I3TH-I4TH CENTURY. MUSEUM OF TURKISH AND ISLAMIC ART, ISTANBUL.

and now in the Ethnographic Museum in Ankara. Its globular body is densely covered with one of the most elaborate and spirited arabesque compositions of the thirteenth century, and is thus related to similar ensembles carved in wood or stone. The technique used here is repoussé, otherwise rarely employed for bronze and brass; however, it was well known to gold- and silversmiths and may for that reason have been used here, for the lamp with its original gilding must have looked very like an object from a jeweler's shop. The body is pierced in many places to allow the passage of the light from an oil lamp which was kept in a glass container within. On its neck the lamp displays a different type of decoration, a *nashki* inscription on a background of winding scrolls; this renders a Koranic passage from the *Sura of Light* (XXIV, 35) which pertains to light as a divine symbol: "Allah is the light of the heavens and the earth; the similitude of His light is as a niche wherein is a lamp, and the lamp is in a glass. The glass is as it were a shining star . . ."

In accordance with this verse, representations of lamps were sometimes carved in the prayer niches of various mosques of the Jazira: and having probably seen such designs, Ali, the bronzeworker (who may have fled into the interior of Anatolia to escape the sack of Nisibis by the Mongols in 1259) alluded to this iconography in his decoration. Although metal lamps with ajour decoration had been used in Iran from the late ninth or early tenth century on, they usually showed only a fret pattern with inserted inscriptions. The Konya lamp is the first of those that have come down to us to employ a much more sophisticated pattern and also the first to inscribe the Koranic "Light Verse" of Sura XXIV. While it was followed in these two respects by later pieces, it remained unique in another aspect; that is, the use of bulls' heads for the three attachments which affix the suspension chains. No other Muslim country was willing to employ such a novel, yet unorthodox feature in a sacred setting, though a similar bull's head occurs also on the façade of the Great Mosque of Diyarbakır.

The Ala eddin Mosque of Konya and that of Eşrefoğlu in Beyşehir have provided us also for the first time with yet another group of mosque furnishings which, in this instance, is particularly precious: three nearly complete and eight fragmentary pile carpets of the thirteenth century, some of them of large dimensions and nearly all of them with different patterns. To this group a prayer carpet mentioned by Ibn Bibi should be added as it represents yet another Seljuk category, although no actual piece has been preserved. These Seljuk pieces represent a much more advanced form of the knotted carpet than the fragments of the third to the sixth century A.D. found in eastern Turkestan which were probably the products of more westerly regions in Central Asia. Since no connection has thus far been established between a still older carpet in Achaemenid style of the fifth or fourth century B.C. found in Pazirik in the Altai Mountains and later examples, these Turkish carpets may, for the time being, be regarded as the oldest fully developed specimens of a technique which came to the Near East with the Seljuks in the eleventh century and later took on enormous proportions there. The various Seljuk carpets already have the general organization that we are accustomed to find in such a product; namely, a field framed by a border which is subdivided into a broad, central stripe and narrow guard stripes along the outer and inner edges. A peculiarity of the Seljuk carpets is the rather small scale of the overall patterns presented in staggered rows within the field in comparison to the much bolder designs in the main part of the border. The field patterns are either outright geometric, or they represent highly stylized floral motifs derived from textiles; but in either case the weavers often introduced hook-like excrescences. The color scheme of five to eight hues is rather somber and shows a predilection for two shades of blue, red, or green. This stark, restrictive aspect, as well as the simplicity and severity of the designs, give these carpets a very strong and monumental appearance. It therefore does not seem surprising that they were greatly admired by Marco Polo in the thirteenth century, and less than a century later, by Ibn Battuta, who specifically attributed them to Aksaray (to the northeast of Konya). However, even in these

BRONZE DOOR KNOCKER. ISLAMISCHE ABTEILUNG, STAATLICHE MUSEEN, BERLIN-DAHLEM.

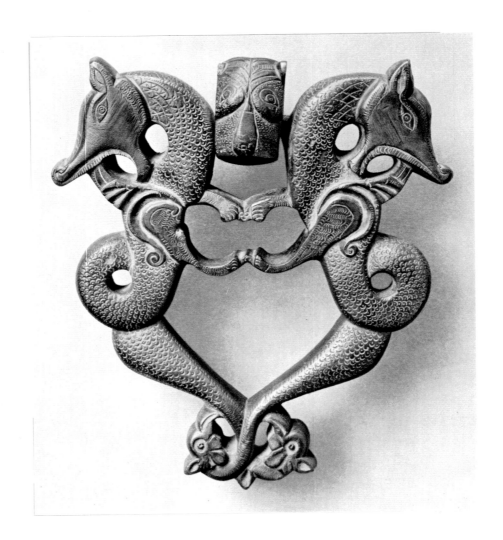

DIVRIĞI, GREAT MOSQUE. STONE CARVING AT THE WEST PORTAL. 1228.

pieces it is possible to point to an unorthodox procedure. From a religious point of view it was not proper to use Arabic letters on a carpet to be stepped upon since they form, so to speak, the raw material for sacred texts; but such lettering was nevertheless either used outright in borders (though always in an ornamental manner and as pseudo-writing) or the straight upper halves of letters with their triangular endings were introduced as ornamental devices. These pseudo-epigraphic borders set a precedent which was followed by the weavers of Turkish carpets of the fifteenth and sixteenth centuries and later by artisans in Iran as well.

Next to the sacred world of mosques and *medreses*, it was the royal palace which formed the main focus of artistic activity. Unfortunately none of the Seljuk palaces are well preserved, nor have extensive excavations been made to give us a better idea of such institutions and particularly of their furnishings. We therefore have to rely mainly on individual, stray objects which have come down to us. Although they usually lack inscriptions and other data which would specifically connect them with one or the other of the Anatolian rulers, they can nevertheless for stylistic reasons be associated with their courts. Thus a very fine bronze door knocker now in the Berlin Museum probably came from a palace. It shows two confronted dragons which look backwards and bite into their wings while their knotted tails end in birds' heads; it was affixed to the door by a stylized head of an animal, perhaps representing a lion head. A very similar door knocker composed of dragons with coiled tails and again held up by a mask-like animal head occurs in the manuscripts on "Automata" by al-Jazari, a work written and composed for the Artuqid Sultan Mahmud in Diyarbakır in 1206. It is therefore very likely that the piece in the Berlin Museum comes from Anatolia. A scarcely known lead piece represents a bird with outstretched wings that apparently once formed the spout of a fountain, similar to the four bronze lions performing the same function at the corners of an ornamental pool which Ibn Battuta saw in the center of the audience hall in the palace of the Sultan of Birgi. The animal is rather stylized, particularly in the formation of the head, which resembles the lion mask of the door knocker; yet the piece is remarkably alive and at the same time very monumental. It appeared in Turkey itself; since its manufacture at a later date, particularly in Ottoman times, is most unlikely, its attribution to the Seljuk period seems reasonable. In any case, it is a remarkable piece of animal sculpture and surpasses in its impressive rendering and in its suggested movement the more inert Fatimid bronze sculptures such as the great griffon from the Campo Santo of Pisa or the Seljuk incense burners in the form of lions or birds from Iran.

A great many pieces of pottery have been found near the old palace structures and during preliminary excavations undertaken there. Unfortunately, most of this material is in fragmentary condition. It is, however, evident that the ceramic industry was very varied and technically of a high standard, although not reaching the quality of the Iranian and Syrian production. These Anatolian pieces followed Persian prototypes,

SILK FABRIC, PROBABLY OF SELJUK ORIGIN. 13TH CENTURY. MUSÉE HISTORIQUE DES TISSUS, LYONS.

even the luxury production of lusterwares and of polychrome, over-glaze-painted vessels and tiles. However, in nearly each instance there is enough diversity in the stylistic handling to reveal the hand of an Anatolian artisan. There was also a secondary influence from Syria, particularly from Rakka wares; but the potter and tile-maker never slavishly copied these models but rather went their own ways.

A great deal of artistic endeavor in the palace was of course focused around the king and various members of the court. A close association with the person of the king is provided by a splendid textile (now in the Musée Historique des Tissus in Lyons) which later was made into a priest's cope. It is a silk which shows as its repeat pattern

INSIDE OF ENAMELLED COPPER BASIN. 12TH CENTURY. FERDINANDEUM, INNSBRUCK.

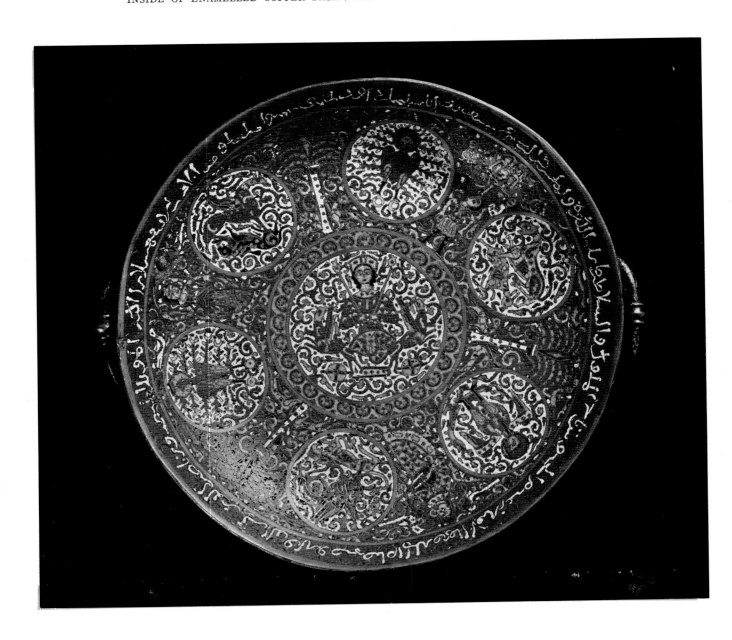

STEEL MIRROR WITH GOLD INLAYS. EARLY 13TH CENTURY. TREASURY OF THE TOPKAPU SARAYI MUSEUM, ISTANBUL.

two closely set, addorsed lions in gold on red ground and placed in circles filled by little rosettes. The areas not taken up by the animals are given over to arabesques which emanate from the animals' mouths and tails, and well-drawn arabesques occur also in the spandrels. The design of two heraldically stylized animals in circles formed by small, round units goes back to the more starkly designed Sasanian textile patterns, but by introducing the arabesques the design has become richer and more varied and the whole appears more fluid. Fortunately part of an inscription has been preserved at one end of the silk which indicates that it was made for the Sultan Ala eddin Kay-Kobad, the son of Kay-Khosrow, probably the first ruler of that name, who ruled from 1220 to 1237. Marco Polo mentioned that Anatolia produced "a great quantity of fine and rich silks of cramorsy and other colors and plenty of other stuffs" while Ibn Bibi often spoke of royal "robes of honor" of three different grades. It seems therefore very likely that this crimson piece not only belonged to the well-known king but was actually made in Anatolia, probably in a royal *tiraz* or workshop for the production of "robes of honor" similar to those established in many Muslim courts. Other textiles cannot be connected as easily with Anatolia, although the use of such common motifs as the double-headed eagle or a combination of four lions with one head (similar to a stone sculpture of two lions with one head on the hall portal of the Alay Han) make an attribution to Anatolia very suggestive.

Another object which could very well be of Rum-Seljuk origin is a gold buckle now in the Berlin Museum which has as its carefully worked decoration two seated, confronted animals looking backwards, the whole set within a polylobed cartouche. On one side the animals used are winged rabbits and on the other, winged, bird-headed quadrupeds, apparently griffons. While there is hardly any doubt that the skillfully stylized animals placed on arabesque ground date from the early thirteenth century and are, in a wider sense, Seljuk work, a good case can also be made for an Anatolian origin. First, we know for certain from Ibn Battuta's account that gold objects were used in the Anatolian courts and furthermore that Rumi's pupil and deputy was called Salah eddin Zarkub ("the gold beater"). In addition, the same fantastic quadrupeds occur again in the framing border of a steel mirror with designs in low relief and further enhanced by fine, hammered-in gold inlays. The general shape of this mirror, now in the Treasury Room of the Topkapu Sarayı Museum, corresponds to one of the two common types of such implements used in Muslim times. This one, having a handle, is of Classical derivation while the other type, with a central, pierced knob, is of Chinese origin. The main subject of the mirror is a cavalier riding to the left and holding a large falcon on his gloved left hand while clasping the reins of his horse with his right. The princely hunter is splendidly dressed in Turkish attire, and his special prominence is further underlined by a halo around his head (which here, as elsewhere in Islamic iconography, does not therefore imply any saintliness). On his chase he is accompanied by a hunting dog which is fastened to his saddle by means of a leash, while a second dog runs loose behind the horse. (This uncommon stress on dogs has its parallel in the reliefs of two pairs of hunting and shepherd dogs on a gateway to the Citadel of Harran dated 1059). The game is indicated by a flying duck to the left of the rider's face. Since there is also a diminutive, snake-like dragon in the lower left, we can assume that, in spite of the main aspect of the scene, the subject actually represents an amalgamation of two themes, that of a "falconer" and of "St George killing the dragon." The animal frieze around the border is a typical device of the Seljuk period which is varied only insofar as the animals are not all running one behind the other in one direction as is usual but are converging on a pair of winged dragons, a commonly used design in Iraq, Syria, and Anatolia which is sometimes of symbolic significance while in other cases possibly heraldic in function. Another unusual aspect in this frieze are the two centaurs which have the aspect of the zodiacal sign Sagittarius. However, there exists an Anatolian parallel as Sagittarius occurs by itself on an Artuqid coin issued in Mardin in 1202. This mirror is again an object which has no exact technical and iconographic parallel anywhere else in the Muslim world. All indications point, however, to Anatolia; and as it was also found there, it is reasonable to attribute it to that country.

At the end of this discussion of medieval-Turkish metalwork two other unusual, if not unique, objects should also be considered both of which have a close connection with Southwest Anatolia. The first, in the Ferdinandeum in Innsbruck, is a two-handled copper bowl densely covered both inside and out with designs in cloisonné enamel in seven colors (red, purple, blue, turquoise, green, white and yellow) with the dividing fillets all originally gilded. According to an Arabic inscription along the outer edge of the interior, it was made for the Artuqid Emir Dawud (1114-1144) whose father had ruled over Mardin and Hisn-Kaifa on the Tigris (the modern Hasankeyf), not too far from the more important city of Diyarbakır which, however, had as yet not been conquered by this dynasty and was still ruled by a Turkish prince of the Inalid family. Dawud's domain centered first around Hisn-Kaifa and he later also occupied Kharput on the Euphrates (to the east of Malatya). The artisan of this prince employed a technique very rarely used in the Islamic world (and then only for jewelry or weapons) which he must have learned from Byzantine sources. The main motif in the center of the bowl, the ascension of Alexander the Great, also came from the same cultural milieu. The great Macedonian appears here as a youthful king holding up hunks of flesh on two staffs so as to lure the two griffons attached to his chariot to carry him heavenwards. Quite obviously Dawud identified himself with the great conqueror and thus implied his own apotheosis; he further underlined this allegory by showing other subjects with a royal connotation in the six framing roundels: a heraldically rendered eagle with a snake in his fangs, two similarly drawn peacocks and three lions attacking a weaker animal. The three symbolical birds have haloes as does the Turkish prince on the gold-inlaid, steel mirror in the Topkapu Sarayı Museum; two of the lions are winged like the rabbits on another royal object, the gold belt buckle in the Berlin Museum. In the spaces between the roundels, three tree-of-life renditions alternate with figures of a bearded lute player, a dancing girl and acrobats performing a balancing act, all of whom are entertainers at the royal court. On the exterior a very similar iconography can be found around the center of the undecorated foot. The roundels now contain besides the symbolical animals two wrestlers and a group comprising a seated lute player and standing *saqi*, that is, a page offering a goblet, while in the interstitial areas we meet again a dancing girl, a lute player and also a flutist. In spite of the specifically given name of the Artuqid ruler, there remains some uncertainty about the origin of this bowl because the Arabic inscription on the interior is given in cursive *nashki* script which, at that time, was known only in the faraway, eastern parts of the Muslim world. As Ibn Bibi speaks, however, of different colored inlays in metal objects used in Anatolia in the thirteenth century, the best solution of this puzzling problem seems to be that at least the inscription (which has two improper inversions in the sequence of words) was made by an East-Iranian craftsman working for the Artuqid court. Be that as it may, we have here a unique object which depicts the royal aspiration of a Turkish prince of the first half of the twelfth century and shows at the same time the various forms of entertainment current at his court.

Different problems are posed by a pair of bronze kettledrums with chased decorations which were found in Diyarbakır and are now in the Museum of Turkish and Islamic Art in Istanbul. The technique and the arabesque scrolls used on these pieces induced one of the greatest authorities in the field, not only to date them "about 1200," but also to call them Khorasan-work, that is, East Persian. However, among the many known products of that province there seem to be no parallels for the same kind of monumental Kufic writing with its human and dragon heads attached to the tall letters and their peculiar loopings. Now that we know from the inscription on the mosque lamp in the Ankara Museum that bronze objects of the highest quality were made in Anatolia in the thirteenth century and as Ibn Bibi speaks also of serving bowls, braziers, incense burners, tripods and writing boxes, it seems unnecessary to assume that such more ordinary objects were brought to Diyarbakır from a region many hundreds of miles to the east, especially as also in many other respects the Anatolian craftsmen showed originality in executing works of art. If this assumption is correct, we would have simple but truly functional objects with skillfully drawn inscriptions and an ornamentation appropriate to the shape; at the same time we would possess a piece of evidence which helps us to visualize the playing of a military band at an Anatolian court or during the warfare waged by one of its rulers when the beating of drums signaled departure and attack, or in the case of victory, general jubilation.

A word might finally be said about the exercise of the art of painting in Anatolia in the thirteenth century. The earliest known work is *The Book of the Knowledge of Mechanical Devices* by an engineer called al-Jazari (and therefore a native of the Jazira region); since 1181, he had worked for the Artuqid sultans of Diyarbakır and was urged in 1206 to write this particular treatise at the instigation of the then-ruling king, Mahmud, the great-grandson of the Dawud, for whom the earlier-described enamel copper bowl had been made. The original Diyarbakır version has not been preserved, only a series of later illustrated renditions, some of which came from the Arab world, especially Egypt, while others were copied even in faraway India. One of these versions, written by a scribe from Hisn-Kaifa in 1254 (652 H.) after a copy of the author's holograph of 1206, is the earliest manuscript to have come down to us (Topkapu Sarayı Museum, Ahmet III, 3472). It probably still represents a fairly good reflection of the original and there are also several other copies of the thirteenth and fourteenth century which help us to further identify the basic iconography although the local styles brought about slight changes in the general treatment. The miniatures are, so to say, artistic blueprints for the construction of vessels suitable for the entertainment of royal guests at banquets, for utensils used for bloodletting and washing, for musical instruments and contrivances for raising water to higher levels and for whatever other mechanical tasks al-Jazari was charged with during his long service. Like the text which goes ultimately back to such Greek writers as Heron and Philon of Byzantium the illustrations, too, are at least iconographically dependent on Classical prototypes, although the figures are clothed in contemporary Muslim garb and painted in the prevailing Muslim style of the period.

While this account of the material culture of Anatolia has dealt mainly with the thirteenth century and particularly with its first half, the grandiose *mihrab* of the Mosque in Damse Köy and the rich and sophisticated illuminations in fourteenth-century manuscripts were at least partial proof of the continued excellence of the arts in the periods of the Emirates before the Sultanate of the Ottomans established its hegemony in Asia Minor. At that time, Anatolia was prosperous through trade. Merchants from Cairo, Alexandria, and Syria visited it; and, as Ibn Battuta informs us, its wood was, for instance, exported to Egypt; its apricots, to Egypt and Syria; and the Aksaray carpets, not only to the Levant but also to Iraq, Turkestan and China. The towns were flourishing, and the same traveler speaks continually of their splendor. Many details point to affluence at the courts; thus, the Sultan of Laranda offered Ibn Battuta fruit and sweetmeats on silver platters and the Sultan of Birgi, gold and silver bowls for sherbet of raisin to be eaten with gold and silver spoons while the Emir of Izmir presented as a gift several large, silver goblets filled with silver coins, as well as horses, garments, and slaves. And as foreboding of events to come, he mentioned that the Sultan Orhan (1332-1359) of the house of Osman residing in Bursa "was the greatest of the Kings of the Turkmens, and the richest in wealth, lands, and military forces."

ISTANBUL, SULTAN AHMED CAMII (THE BLUE MOSQUE OF SULTAN AHMED I). INTERIOR VIEW. 1609-1617.

THE OTTOMANS

Even more extraordinary than the rise and flowering of the Seljuk Sultanate of Rum is the development of the princely house of Osman and its followers, called Osmanlı in Turkish and the Ottomans in the West.

The emirate of Osman began as one of the smallest of the ten principalities which were the result of the breakdown of the central government in Konya, but being geographically closest to the seat of Byzantine Imperial power it also faced the greatest historical challenge and by dint of valor and religious fervor successfully responded to it. It became the most important ghazi state, where warriors were zealously fighting "the holy war" against the infidels in Western Anatolia. Soon after 1340 when nearly all the Asiatic possessions of Byzantium had been taken, special circumstances opened the way for an eventual conquest of the Balkans and other sections of southeastern Europe, as well as of other parts of Anatolia. In 1354 Ottoman soldiers were called to Thrace to fight as auxiliaries in an internal struggle within the Greek Empire. This led, in 1384, to the ceding of Gallipoli as a base for these troops and it was from here that their own European campaigns started. In 1361 Murad I (1362-1389) conquered Adrianople which, as Edirne, became the European capital of the Ottomans and was kept as second capital even after the eventual conquest of Constantinople. Campaigns in Macedonia, Bulgaria, and Serbia led to the great battle of Kosovo Polje in 1389 which finally subdued the Serbian kingdom.

In the same period the Ottomans extended their domain toward the East. In 1354, in addition to acquiring Gallipoli they conquered Ankara, then a well-established and flourishing Muslim town. This was followed by the incorporation of several emirates, either by military action or peaceful efforts, so that by 1400 the fourth Ottoman ruler Bayazid I, called Yildirim, "the Thunderbolt" (1389-1402), controlled nearly all of Anatolia. He had himself invested as Sultan of Rum by the Abbasid shadow caliph residing in Cairo and this action officially proclaimed him the successor of the Seljuks. He even tried to achieve what was thought to be an event of almost eschatological significance, the conquest of Constantinople, though the siege proved unsuccessful.

These imperial ambitions eventually clashed with those of the other leading figure of the East, the great conqueror Timur Leng (known in Europe as Tamerlane), who defeated Bayazid near Ankara in 1402. After a series of critical years made more difficult by a war of succession, followed by a period of consolidation under Mehmet I, the latter's son Murad II (1421-1451) resumed an expansionist European policy by renewed campaigns in the Balkans during which he also repeatedly battled the Hungarians, who from now on were the great Western defenders against the Turkish onslaught in Europe. About 1420 this same ruler also instituted a most successful scheme for making the Christian countries provide the state with the best of their human resources, at the same time securing the material for a professional army and civil service completely loyal to the sultan. This is the *devshirme* or levy of boys who were regularly recruited from the conquered Christian population, then converted to Islam and Turkicized during a special training period. The military branch of this corps constitutes the janissaries (actually *yeni cheri*, or "new soldiers"). The janissaries formed the infantry and were the core of the army which made all the subsequent conquests possible; they proved to be the mainstay of Turkish power, though in later times they frequently became undisciplined and mutinied, until finally in 1826 they had to be dissolved.

The crowning military and political achievement of Turkish expansion was accomplished by Murad's son, Mehmet II (1451-1481) whose greatest feat gave him the title of Fatih, "the Conqueror." While still a youth of about twenty he concluded a thoroughly prepared and ingeniously conducted land and sea siege lasting fifty days, which on May 29, 1453, led to the storming of the valiantly defended, though greatly weakened city of Constantinople, and by this deed to the collapse of the Byzantine Empire. The Asiatic and European parts of the Ottoman Sultanate were now united and the Sultan of Rum became the successor of the last Greek Emperor, Constantine XI Palaeologus Dragases, who was slain. During the remainder of his reign Mehmet fought continuously, both in Europe and Asia, and in this way consolidated and rounded off his realm.

Mehmet's grandson, Yavuz Selim I, "the Grim" (1512-1520) conquered further immense areas and added new luster to the house of Osman. In the battle of Chaldiran (1514) he defeated Shah Ismail of Iran, his neighbor to the east, and for a while even occupied his capital Tabriz. This campaign was not only conducted for military and political reasons, but had religious significance as well, for the Persian Shi'ite form of Islam was anathema to the orthodox beliefs of the strictly Sunnite Ottoman ruler who had severely suppressed Shi'ism in Anatolia. However, neither this sultan nor any of his successors was able to conquer the whole of the Iranian plateau although they continued to regard the Shi'ites "as more different and less holy than even the Christians," as a grand vizier explained to the Hapsburg Ambassador van Busbeck. Selim was more successful in the West by first conquering Syria and then crushing its ruler in Egypt (1515-1517). Shortly after the conquest of Cairo and the execution of its Mamluk sultan he received the keys of the Ka'ba in Mecca, the central shrine of Islam, thus becoming the protector of the two holy cities in Arabia, Mecca and Medina. He further buttressed his Islamic prestige by taking for himself the title of *khalifa* or caliph (that is, "successor or vice-regent of the Prophet Muhammed"). This was an immensely bold and significant step, especially as now for the first time this hallowed position was vested in a non-Arab sovereign, in whose family it was to remain till 1924.

The apogee of Turkish power was reached during the long reign of Selim's son Süleyman I (1520-1566), called Kanuni, "the Lawgiver," by the Turks and "the Magnificent" by the West. It was at this time that Turkey more than ever before came into conflict with Central European forces and by wars and an alliance with France participated in European power politics. Early in his reign Süleyman conquered Belgrade (1521) and took the island of Rhodes from the Knights of St John (1522) who then moved to Malta. From 1526 to 1533 there was a continuous expansion at the northern frontier which led successively to the defeat of Louis of Hungary in the battle of Mohacs (1526) and the consequent end of his kingdom, the first conquest of Buda (Budapest) in 1529 and two weeks after this event to the first Turkish siege of Vienna. The siege had to be given up after fourteen days, as the Turkish army did not have sufficient supplies; however Süleyman continued his struggle with the Hapsburgs, especially with Ferdinand of Austria, over Hungary and Transylvania. At the same time Süleyman's admiral Kheireddin Barbarossa, a former corsair, waged a long-drawn-out successful naval war against Spain for the control of the Western Mediterranean and raided the coast of North Africa, Sicily, Southern Italy, and Dalmatia. Venetian settlements in the Aegean Sea as far as Crete were lost to the Turks. In the East, Baghdad and Iraq were conquered and for a while even the Iranian capital Tabriz and the surrounding province of Azerbaijan were occupied (1534). Later the Turkish fleet extended its control to the Red Sea, thereby taking Yemen and Aden and even penetrating the Indian Ocean. Only Malta withstood the Turks, and, for a while, the Hungarian fortress of Szigetvar also resisted their onslaught. It was during the siege of the last-named stronghold that Süleyman died, two days before the final conquest. Although Turkish arms also gained great victories later on, they were never again able to achieve so many successes on such widely different fronts.

In view of this fact it seems worthwhile to quote here a statement made by the Imperial Ambassador van Busbeck in one of his *Letters*, as it succinctly gives the reason for the many victories in the far-reaching campaigns undertaken by Süleyman: "On their side are the limitless resources of the Turkish Empire, unbroken strength, the knowledge of and experience with weapons, soldiers of long service, the sureness of victory, perseverance, perfect accord, order, discipline, unpretentiousness and watchfulness. On our side poverty of the state, private extravagance, reduced vigor, broken courage, an insufficient will to exert oneself, lack of experience with weapons, inadequate soldiers, greedy officers, contempt of discipline, dissoluteness, carelessness, drunkenness, immoderation in eating, and worst of all,—they are used to gaining victories, we to being vanquished."

The name by which Süleyman's son Selim II (1566-1574) is known, "the Sot," indicates for the first time the beginnings of deterioration of the moral fiber in the house of Osman, and this hint is corroborated by the fact that this sultan left the running of his empire to his grand vizier. There were still successes, such as the conquest of

BURSA, YESHIL CAMII (THE GREEN MOSQUE). 1419-1424. VIEW OF EXTERIOR.

The Green Mosque represents a high-water mark of early Ottoman architecture, although owing to the death of Mehmet I in 1421 the building was never fully completed and thus lacks the clearly envisaged portico. Being the logical development of mosques built in or near Bursa by Orhan I (1339), Murad I (1366), and Bayazid I (1391-1395), the Green Mosque was the final adaptation of the medrese scheme for communal prayer. It unified the public area by eliminating the cells between the eyvans (a solution never tried in Iran) and clearly separated the four corner rooms that serve secondary purposes. It also introduced a sultan's lodge above the entrance eyvan where the ruler could—much like the Byzantine Empress in St Sophia—perform his prayer in a well-protected place, thus doing away with the architecturally disturbing royal box next to the mihrab. Other outstanding features of this mosque are the carvings in the harmonious marble façade and the ceramic and painted decorations—all of which bear out Evliya Chelebi's statement: "In no other land have travelers seen a place of worship like this."

Chios from the Genoese and of Cyprus from the Venetians (1570-1571) but the Holy Alliance of the Pope, Venice, and Spain under the leadership of Don Juan of Austria finally defeated the Turkish navy at Lepanto (1571), an event that made a profound impression on the contemporary Western mind. A seesaw pattern of victories and defeats, of gains and losses now becomes the rule, and though the Turks were on the offensive till the end of the seventeenth century (Peace of Passarowitz, 1699), the balance turned slowly in favor of the West. However, the Turks held most of their major possessions in southeastern Europe, North Africa and Asia until the late nineteenth and early twentieth century. The excesses and mental deterioration of some sultans, the inexperienced youth of others, and the pernicious influence of the harem and of drink contributed to the general decline. Even more serious were the revolts of the janissaries and corrupt administrations, as well as the unwieldiness of the enormous empire with its many heterogeneous nationalities and religions and, finally, the constant interference of the European powers in Turkish affairs. However, the details of this long-drawn-out struggle which led to the final dismemberment of the empire are beyond the scope of this book. It was the tremendous momentum given by the great personalities and events of the fifteenth and sixteenth centuries which continued to be felt in the subsequent centuries and left an indelible imprint on the arts.

Although there is a genetic connection between the classic Islamic architecture and its Rum-Seljuk variations on the one hand and Ottoman buildings on the other, the latter are so remarkably transformed that they represent a class by themselves which has given a characteristic imprint to the physical aspect and especially the skyline of the cities and towns of the Turkish Empire from the middle of the fourteenth century on. Another important fact is the continued eagerness to try out new forms which persisted in a limited way even after the basic structural ideas had been established under Bayazid II about 1501.

The Bursa era and the first half-century of building activity in Constantinople represent the experimental period. However, even then the paramount theme of Ottoman architecture—a single dome or a sequence of domes—appears in various schemes and was continuously used, becoming still more prominent in the later great buildings of Constantinople. The best known of the early hypostyle mosques, the Ulu Jami or Great Mosque of Bursa (1396-1399), is covered with twenty domes, though it continues the Seljuk fashion of substituting an internal court with a fountain for the outer court of Arab structures. The traditional scheme with an external courtyard exists also, though here, too, the sanctuary is covered either by one large dome or a succession of domes or eventually in the most advanced example of the pre-Constantinopolitan period, the Uç Sherefli Mosque in Edirne of 1447, by one large central dome with two small lateral ones. In addition there are also cases of single dome structures dating from as early as 1335, these being usually preceded by a portico, a novel and soon very popular element in Ottoman architecture.

Still more important and characteristic for this period is the "inverted T scheme" used mainly for mosques beginning with the Mosque of Sultan Orhan of 1339 in Bursa and occasionally also for other building types. It combines the longitudinal direction of the Seljuk basilica-type mosque (which is otherwise given up) with the Seljuk *medrese*, whose court is covered by a dome. In these buildings, which are probably inspired by Byzantine prototypes, the sanctuary *eyvan* in the rear projects beyond the rectangular block of the structure, while the entrance *eyvan* is much reduced and preceded by a portico. The side *eyvans* may open onto the court but can also be walled off, enabling their rooms to serve as quarters for religious devotees, as a hostel, or as schoolrooms. All the parts are usually domed, the main axis being formed by the dome over the sanctuary *eyvan* and the still higher dome over the former court, whose floor is usually on a lower level and which still houses a fountain. The façade is organized by lateral *mihrabs* and various windows in two stories; in the center of these the now better-integrated entrance with its traditional *muqarnas* half-dome forms the main axis. The ceramic decoration is still very conspicuous, although it differs both in the techniques used and in the range of colors from the Seljuk faience mosaics. Thus the *cuerda secca* (or dry cord) technique now becomes popular; here the various glazes are separated by outlines made with a purple pigment mixed with a greasy substance which burns out in the firing and is sufficient to prevent the bleeding of the different colors. The main colors are cobalt, blue, two greens, a strong yellow and white. Besides the traditional arabesques and inscriptions, now usually executed in yellow or gold to render a large, bold cursive script called *sulus*, there are also floral motifs of Chinese derivation, especially peonies.

The main example for all these new architectural and decorative features is the Green Mosque built over a period of more than four years (1419-1424) in Bursa, whose splendor its builder, Sultan Mehmet I, describes in the following terms: "This noble shrine, the creation of the Creator of Nature, the product of the Maker of Beings, is a copy of the garden of well-being (that is, of Paradise) which was made by the decree of the Almighty and All-Knowing; it is one of the fields of the Hereafter which was created with the splendor of this world; it proudly extends in all directions, leaving large cities behind in utter perplexity—indeed, God did not bless with a similar work all the ages since the revolving canopy of heaven was first set in motion . . ."

The grandiose, deep-colored and extremely rich, though well-composed and sophisticated ceramic decorations of the *mihrab*, the various lodges, *eyvans*, and side rooms are linked by dadoes of ultramarine and green hexagonal wall tiles with golden designs. According to inscriptions, the all-over architectural and ornamental design of the Green Mosque was due to the architect Hajji Ivaz, son of Akhi Bayazid, who had the support of the master decorator Ali, son of Ilyas Ali, and of tile workers from Tabriz; their work represents one of the high-water marks of architectural design and ceramic decoration. Fortunately, there is in the same town still another contemporary and equally splendid monument by the same architect working with an artisan from Tabriz; it is the "Green Türbe" containing the monumental cenotaph of Mehmet I (who died in 1421) and other members of his family, all covered with exquisite tiles, as are the entrance gate, the *mihrab*, the lunettes over windows and doors, and the side walls.

A slightly later but equally important building is the Mosque of Murad II built in 1436 in Edirne, the European capital of the Ottomans. This mosque contains another richly decorated polychrome *mihrab* in which white *sulus* inscriptions and arabesques stand out sharply against the deep blue background and other secondary ornamental elements in yellow. More significant in view of later developments are the underglaze-painted hexagonal blue and white wall tiles apparently made by Syrian artisans or at least under strong Syrian influence. Here formal arrangements of lotus and peony designs in the Chinese manner of the middle of the fourteenth century are combined with other units decorated with more realistically treated Near Eastern motifs such as a cypress tree and swirling leaf sprays. This same color scheme and the same two aspects of the floral design were used for the decoration of vessels, plates and lamps later in the century with the freer Islamic motifs finally predominating.

Other traditional building types continue to be used in the pre-Constantinopolitan period, again with specific changes. Thus the lateral confines of the *medrese* are occupied by the students' cells, only rarely interrupted by much reduced *eyvans*. The dominating feature in these *medreses* is the large, domed *eyvan* in the rear. The *türbe* is also domed with the dome resting on columns or piers in the center of a square building or else directly over a square, hexagonal or octagonal structure. There are a few new architectural types, especially the *imaret* or kitchen for the poor, of which the oldest preserved example follows the "inverted T scheme"; this was built by Murad I in memory of his mother Nilufer Hatun in 1388. Novel, too, is the idea of constructing a *külliye* or complex of public buildings, first realized by Bayazid I in Bursa in 1398 and finished after his death in 1403; the walled-in area includes two gateways, a mosque, *medrese*, the royal *türbe*, a fountain, *imaret*, *hammam* (or public bath), an aqueduct, and a small royal palace. Nearby were also a hospital (following the contemporary *medrese* scheme), a dervish monastery and a caravanserai which have almost entirely disappeared although their existence is vouched for by the deed of the founder.

This large-scale agglomeration of buildings of various types forms from that period on a characteristic aspect of Ottoman urban architecture and the idea continues to grow and to include still other structures like medical schools, insane asylums and libraries. Such undertakings presupposed financial and administrative planning on a large scale as the deeds of gift specify all the employees and their salaries down to the lavatory attendants and cleaners of sewers. These buildings were, moreover, impressive not only from an architectural point of view but also for the public and scientific spirit which they embodied. For instance, the seventeenth-century Turkish traveler Evliya Chelebi has this to say about a novel treatment of the insane by means of music: "I noted something curious in his foundation grant. His Majesty Bayazid II appointed three singers, as well as a flutist, a violinist, a flageolet player, a cymbalist, a harpist and a lutanist to provide therapy for the sick, to improve the suffering, to strengthen the spirit of the insane and to reduce the bile. They come three times a week and play their music in front of the sick and insane. By the grace of the Almighty many of them feel relieved..."

While the architecture and especially the tile production speak for a sophisticated, artistic sense and fine craftsmanship, it must be said at the stage of our present knowledge that the other forms of the decorative arts during the greater part of the fifteenth century are not on the same high level. The early pottery vessels (formerly called "Miletus ware") now known to have been made in Iznik are at times free and sketchy in decoration and at times more elaborate, but in neither case can they be regarded as refined wares. However, they are no longer dependent on Persian and Syrian models and constitute an early Ottoman type. The only other medium of which we have more information are the knotted carpets. Though only one piece has been found in Anatolia (now in the Museum in Konya), two large fragmentary pieces have appeared, one in an Italian and the other in a Swedish church, while some related fragments have been unearthed in the ruins of Fustat, a forerunner of Cairo. These geographically scattered finds bear out the statement of Ibn Battuta that the Anatolian carpets of his time were widely exported (see above p. 160). All these pieces and many representations in Italian paintings of the fourteenth and fifteenth centuries show highly conventionalized animals such as birds and quadrupeds, especially lions, placed either in square frames with beveled corners or in rows. The color sometimes changes from animal to animal or from square to square, though it can also remain the same; some carpets show groups of animals such as birds on either side of a tree or animal combats. The Italian paintings provide some clues for localizing and dating these pieces. They were probably produced in western Anatolia, whence they could easily be exported to Europe and Egypt. They were first made in the late thirteenth century and became very popular and numerous in the fourteenth and fifteenth.

The best known example of this category is a large fragment in the Berlin Museum showing a repeat pattern in which a stylized dragon is fighting with a stylized phoenix. Both of these animals derive from the Chinese repertory; however, in China they represent good omens and for that reason Far Eastern objects hardly ever show them in combat, although they can, of course, occur separately on the same piece as they for instance do on a blue and white vase of 1351 A.D. in the Percival David Collection in London. This attitude of combat can only be explained by the changed symbolic significance of the two animals in the Near East where they stand for hostile versus friendly powers and are therefore shown fighting one another. The same general design occurs on the fresco of the *Marriage of the Foundlings* painted by Domenico di Bartolo

ANIMAL CARPET WITH THE REPEAT PATTERN OF A PHOENIX FIGHTING A DRAGON.
ANATOLIA, BEGINNING OF THE 15TH CENTURY.
ISLAMISCHE ABTEILUNG, STAATLICHE MUSEEN, BERLIN-DAHLEM.

The new spaciousness and height of the centralized mosques demanded another focal point since the mihrab's limited concavity in one of the four half-niches was hardly enough. This role was taken over by the mimber which was now of marble or other valuable material and of monumental proportions. However, the richly carved arabesque panels which had been inserted into the Seljuk pulpit disappeared and only allover star designs form the decorative pattern. Also, just as extensive fenestration had reduced the heaviness of the enclosing walls, so now did widely cut-out areas in the mimber walls lighten its massiveness.

ISTANBUL, SHEHZADE CAMII (THE MOSQUE OF THE PRINCE). 1544-1548.

EDIRNE, SELIMIYE CAMII (THE MOSQUE OF SULTAN SELIM II). 1569-1575.

between 1440 and 1444 in the Spedale della Scala in Siena. This fact places the Berlin piece at least in the early part of the fifteenth century. As the design is also to be found on two other Italian paintings and on another small original fragment discovered in Fustat, this pattern must have been fairly common.

After the conquest of Constantinople in 1453 Ottoman art changes in very specific ways, though not immediately. This is demonstrated by the various mosques built in the new capital during the second half of the fifteenth century which all follow earlier Ottoman schemes. However, the great Imperial Church of Hagia Sophia, which had been turned into a mosque called Aya Sofya immediately after the conquest, had a seminal influence. Quite naturally its beauty greatly impressed the conquerors whose architecture had all along explored the artistic possibilities of the dome. A contemporary Ottoman official and writer, Tursun Beg, has left us a description that reflects this admiring attitude:

> If you seek Paradise, Oh you Sufi,
> The topmost heaven is Aya Sofya.

From his further comments it is clear that the impact of the building was due to its immense dome, width, and vast interior:

"What a dome, that vies in rank with the nine spheres of heaven! In this work a perfect master displayed the whole of the architectural science. With half-domes one upon the other, with angles both acute and obtuse, with peerless vaults, like the arched brows of heart-ravishing girls, with stalactite adornments, he made the interior so vast, that it can hold 50,000 persons . . ." (Translation by Bernard Lewis).

Just as the builders of the early Islamic period tried in the late seventh and the first half of the eighth century to emulate and surpass the Christian buildings of Syria, Ottoman architects in Constantinople and other cities of the Empire strove to equal Aya Sofya. The first to take up the challenge was Bayazid II. In 1501, after earlier attempts in Amasya and Edirne, he built the mosque bearing his name in Constantinople. This is an impressive building, though it is smaller and simpler than Aya Sofya whose general scheme of a large, central dome and two half-domes in the longitudinal direction and side aisles it otherwise follows. It remained for the genius of Sinan (1490-1588), the most productive and imaginative architect of the sixteenth century, not only eventually to reach the measurements of the great prototype but to adapt it for Muslim usage. Sinan wrestled with the problem for many decades. In the Shehzade Mosque of 1548 he accomplished what he called his "test as apprentice," creating a fully centralized space with half-domes on all four sides of the central dome whose interior is full of light. Its logical solution of the architectural problem made this in turn the model for several of the great mosques of Constantinople, particularly for that of Sultan Ahmed I of 1617—a building unique in certain respects such as the use of six minarets on the corners of the sanctuary and courtyard and of four tremendous, polylobed pillars in the interior to support the high dome; distinctive also is the special coloristic note given by blue and white tiles above a marble dado.

Bigger than Sinan's Shehzade Mosque is the majestic Mosque of Süleyman the Magnificent of 1557. It is set on an enclosed terrace which contains also the *türbe* of the Sultan and his favorite Sultana, famed even in the West under the name of Roxelana; nearby is a vast complex of dependent structures such as *medreses*, a hospital, soup kitchen, caravanserai, bath and so on. This mosque follows on a larger scale the scheme used for the Mosque of Bayazid II, but its span of 87 feet still did not quite reach the 101½ feet of the sixth-century church. The spatial impression of the interior is also quite different, the Süleymaniye being noteworthy for the high curve of its dome, the large number of smaller domes covering the aisles and their varied size and rhythmic arrangement, and also for the two smaller half-domes which are placed at the sides of the large half-domes, thereby giving the greatest possible extension to the central nave. The exterior represents the epitome of mosque structure in Istanbul. The beautifully finished grey stone masonry is nearly devoid of decoration and produces its masterful effect first of all by the skillful arrangement of domes and buttresses all surrounding the high central dome; this massive, mountainlike core with its different but physically and structurally related parts composed of rounded earth-hugging forms is then juxtaposed to the slender, sharply pointed minarets all poised toward the heavens. No wonder (as Van Busbeck tells us) that the great Sultan placed the finishing of "this truly magnificent and resplendent work" in his lifetime as the first of three wishes; and that its silhouette above the Golden Horn still dominates the skyline of Istanbul as seen from ancient Pera (now called Beyoğlu). Yet Sinan regarded it only as "the work of a journeyman."

Sinan's final accomplishment which surpasses in ingenuity all his 318 structures is the Mosque of Selim II in Edirne. In being able to build a dome of a diameter of 102½ feet and therefore slightly surpassing the minimum diameter of Aya Sofya he had successfully met the basic challenge of the Byzantine model. In addition by supporting the central dome upon eight columns and by placing the better correlated half-domes in the four corners he had avoided the dead, unrelated corner domes of earlier mosques. This arrangement resulted also in a latitudinal structure which was more in line with the traditional Muslim scheme for a mosque. On the outside the building shows the same uncluttered clarity evident in the interior. Its large well-integrated central block culminates in the large dome and is framed by four elegant minarets, whose three balconies are reached by three separate internal staircases. No wonder that Sinan regarded this mosque as his "masterpiece" and that Lady Mary Wortley Montagu after an attentive visit declared (in a letter written on May 17, 1717) this mosque to be "the noblest building she ever saw" and that after having seen "some other mosques built much after the same manner" she found them "not comparable in point of

TILE PANEL WITH CHINESE FLOWERS AND ANIMALS. IZNIK, ABOUT 1540. SÜNNET ODASI, TOPKAPU PALACE, ISTANBUL.

On another contemporary tile nearby the two ch'i-lins at the bottom are replaced by a tall vase from which the vegetation emanates. This reflects an iconography developed from the verse of the *Sura of Light* found on the Seljuk bronze lamp in Ankara (see page 154). In early mihrabs and still on some seventeenth-century carpets the niches contained lamps symbolizing divine light, but the significance of the design was at times forgotten and the motif turned into a beautiful but meaningless decoration.

magnificence ... which is infinitely beyond any church in Germany or England." Altogether Sinan's building shows the logical culmination of a development which started with the Seljuk *medreses* centering around a domed court and then led to the domed mosques of the "inverted T scheme" and the single dome structures of the Bursa period. At the same time it demonstrates again the creative manner in which artistic stimuli were taken up in the Turkish state, not to be slavishly copied but to be creatively reinterpreted for the special demands of its civilization. In a way, one can say that the transformed idea of Aya Sofya is the artistic counterpart of the devshirme system in which the Christian elements of the population were likewise made to serve Ottoman purposes.

Among the secular buildings the palaces are the most important. However, of early structures only one pavilion called "Chinili Köshk" or the Kiosk with Ceramic Decorations built during Mehmet the Conqueror's reign in 1472 has been preserved. It has basically a cruciform scheme within a square centering around a central dome, with four corner rooms and a projecting pentagonal chamber in the back which are also covered by domes. As a delightful special feature of its exterior it presents a high portico resting on a low open base which gives an elegant airiness to the façade. As its name implies, the interior of the building and the entrance *eyvan* are richly decorated with ceramic tilework; this consists of polychrome faience mosaic, colored brick mosaic and hexagonal wall tiles with painted gold ornamentation and thus incorporates both Seljuk and early Ottoman features. All during the later development ceramic wall coverings were to remain an important feature in both sacred and secular structures. As such buildings are numerous and most of them dated or datable, we are fairly well informed about the development of the tile production and also of the closely related manufacture of vessels which likewise took place in Iznik. It seems therefore appropriate to deviate at this point from our architectural discussion in order to consider this twofold ceramic production.

Ever since craftsmen, probably of Syrian origin, had introduced Chinese motifs into the wall tiles of the Mosque of Murad II in Edirne in 1436, the "chinoiserie" element had been important in Ottoman tiles and pottery. In its purest and possibly highest form it is represented by a very large, one-piece panel of about 1540 which was taken from an earlier, now unknown location and in 1641 (or before) reused on the corridor wall of the Sünnet Odası or Circumcision Chamber of the Topkapu Palace. In a niche-shaped field painted under the glaze in blue and turquoise on a white ground, tall stems carrying lanceolated leaves, palmette and rosette flowers are rendered as if tossed by a heavy wind; it is not a pure floral arrangement since two Chinese fantastic animals called *chʻi-lins* are found at the foot of the composition. They, too, are portrayed in agitated postures, biting into leafy branches; one of them turns backward at the same time as if something had aroused its suspicion. In addition, the composition is further enriched by five birds which are placed within the foliage and blend well into it.

In the spandrels at either side of the niche head the potter reserved on a dark blue ground another basically Far Eastern motif: floating ribbons of uneven width which ultimately go back to Chinese cloud bands but had become a popular Ottoman pattern by the beginning of the sixteenth century. The Far Eastern aspect of this tile and of other chinoiserie pieces is acknowledged by Turkish writers, who called such floral designs *Hatayi* (after the Turkish term for China which corresponds to our "Cathay"); however, the addition of turquoise as a second color and the dynamic arrangement is peculiarly Ottoman. In spite of the fact that chinoiserie elements had been in use for over a hundred years this panel is in no way a "late" product with signs of technical or stylistic deterioration. This is made clear by a comparison with a copy of the composition made about 1639 for the Baghdad Köshk of the Topkapu Palace; at that time the tile had to be made in seven sections, the colors have become dull and the white ground has lost its brilliance.

An earlier Turkish phase of the blue and white style in pottery production is exemplified by two vessels in the Topkapu Sarayı Museum, whose designs, curiously enough, prove to have a pronounced Turkish character. In a platter of the end of the fifteenth or the beginning of the sixteenth century, the traditionally Islamic arabesque leaf as well as the Near Eastern version of the Chinese cloud band are the main motifs, while the accompanying Hatayi flowers play only a secondary role. All three together form, however, a well-balanced, beautifully spaced composition whose abstract elements are full of motion and present various contrasts of shapes and outlines. The Islamic character of a mosque lamp is even more pronounced. Here the Hatayi flowers appear only in a narrow zone above the foot, otherwise the loosely spaced designs consist of arabesques, cloud bands and cartouches with Arabic inscriptions. The latter are, as always, more than mere "decoration." In the larger units on the body they present the words "Allah-Muhammad-Ali," a combination which is unusual in Turkey, while the polylobed medallions on the neck contain invocations to Ali. Whereas the trinitarian aspect of the main inscription may very well have had an evident significance in a city with a vast Christian population, its pronounced championship of Ali, the foremost *imam* or spiritual leader of the Shi'ites, implies a date of manufacture before the anti-Shi'ite actions leading to the battle of Chaldiran in 1514. The shape of this mosque lamp is the same which had been used in Seljuk times; however, the original perforations of the metallic versions have been deleted, as they were difficult to apply in the ceramic medium, with the result that all the light is directed upward to be then reflected from the ceiling.

The great demands made on the Iznik potters in the years after 1545 to provide tiles for the restoration of the exterior of the oldest shrine of Islam, the Dome of the Rock in Jerusalem (originally built in 691), led subsequently, from 1555 to 1620, to a vast extension of the production of wall tiles. At the same time the artisans of Iznik succeeded for the first time anywhere in producing after a short experimental period

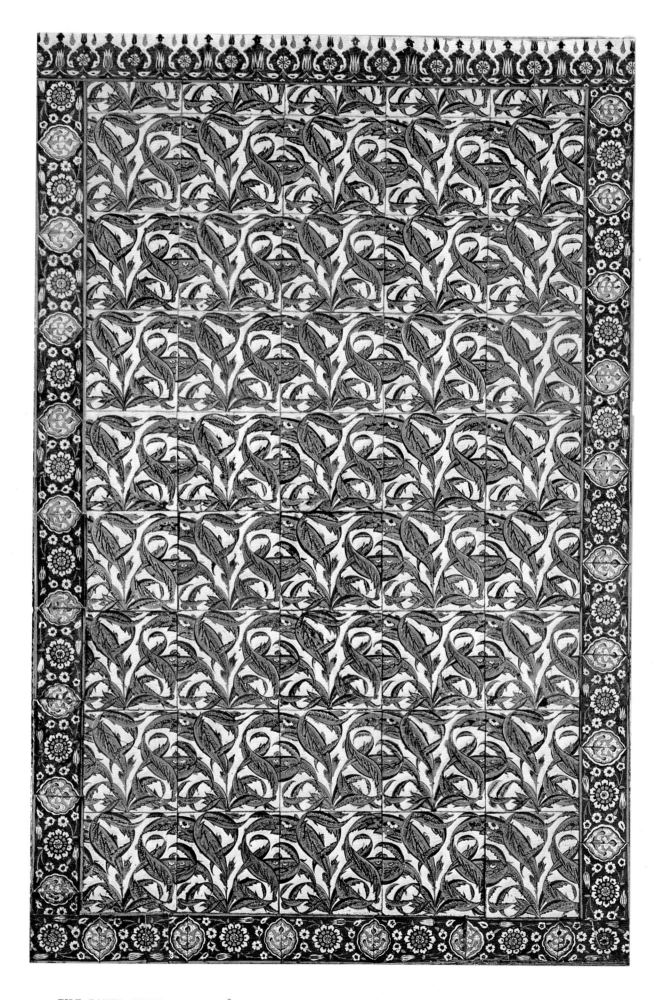

TILE PANEL. IZNIK, ABOUT 1561. RUSTAM PASHA CAMII (MOSQUE OF RUSTAM PASHA), ISTANBUL.

POTTERY LAMPSHADE FROM THE SOKOLLU MEHMET PASHA MOSQUE. IZNIK, EARLY 16TH CENTURY. TOPKAPU SARAYI MUSEUM, ISTANBUL.

a reliable scarlet or sealing-wax red of great brilliance. This was obtained from a ferruginous clay called Armenian bole which had been known since medieval times for its medicinal properties; when applied thickly to tiles and vessels, it produced a noticeable relief effect but even these raised areas were covered by the protective glaze. The addition of this bright color greatly improved the effectiveness of the ceramic palette which had already been further enlarged by various shades of blues and greens as well as black and purple, all usually set against a brilliant white background. A third distinguishing feature was the use of realistically rendered and precisely drawn tulips, carnations, roses, bluebells, hyacinths and other flowers, often in combination with palmettes and long lanceolated leaves with dentated edges set on curving or coiling stems. All of these reflect the great admiration, one might even say the cult, of flowers that flourished at the imperial court and throughout the country, as Van Busbeck at once noted when he was on his way to Constantinople. In addition there were formal arrangements of rosettes, medallions and figures of a slightly more geometrical character. As we know from edicts issued by the imperial offices, the designs were drawn after patterns sent from Constantinople, then probably transferred to the plain tiles by means of pierced stencils and powdered charcoal. In nearly all of these tiles the pattern is larger than the space provided by the individual square or rectangular unit; the complete, continuous design is therefore brought out by the combination of adjacent units which cover the surfaces like a textile. The brilliant glazes and the cheerful harmony of the polychrome palette against the white background combined to create a characteristic air of pervading brightness and gaiety. The outstanding early example of this style dating from 1561 is the Mosque of Rustam Pasha, the Grand Vizier and son-in-law of Süleyman the Magnificent. Here its tiles cover not only the walls and columns of the interior but also the outside wall protected by the usual portico.

The same color scheme and floral repertory which characterized the Iznik tile production of 1555 to 1620 is also to be found on vessels of various types which for a long time were erroneously called "Rhodian." An early example is a tall lamp which once graced the Mosque of Selim II's Grand Vizier Sokollu Mehmet Pasha in Constantinople (built in 1571). This lamp still shows a theme current in the 1550's, the formal arrangement of arabesques on the three circular excrescences of the lower part, which is also decorated with a few bold leaf designs. This decoration is set in juxtaposition to a large inscription with the profession of the Muslim faith rendered in *sulus* writing. The elongated shape indicates a change from the squatter and more accentuated outline of the lamps of the early sixteenth century, which had been painted only in blue and white. The full flavor of the finest pottery production of this category which falls in the period 1560 to 1580 is seen on a platter from the Topkapu Sarayı Museum. The main design is here composed of a variety of flowers which seem to be growing in natural fashion and yet fill gracefully the round concave area. This is framed by the wave and rock pattern typical for the shape. The only unusual feature is the graceful bird within the foliage, as the potter's repertory only occasionally included animals or ships, and human beings almost never. While this production shares the perfect technique, rich polychromy and precise drawing found in other branches of Ottoman art, its lighthearted elegance and natural grace are its own unique quality. No wonder that from the time of manufacture this pottery has been much admired by the West and widely collected. Like pieces of Ming porcelain certain Iznik jugs and tankards have been augmented with sixteenth-century European silver-gilt mounts, while other pieces made to special order were decorated with the coats of arms of noble families. This high prestige has continued to our own time and is voiced in probably the most objective terms by the words of the late Arthur Lane, the finest judge of Near Eastern pottery: "This tilework, with the associated vessels, is among the most astounding achievements in the whole range of the potter's art . . . It is an indigenous ceramic industry more original and more productive than any other of the Islamic wares since the fourteenth century." But alas, the production of Iznik deteriorated in the course of the seventeenth century; the pigment became muddy, the outlines blurred and the white background discolored; by the eighteenth century it was extinct.

POTTERY PLATE WITH BIRD AMONG FLOWERS. IZNIK, ABOUT 1580. TOPKAPU SARAYI MUSEUM, ISTANBUL.

POTTERY LAMPSHADE FROM THE SOKOLLU MEHMET PASHA MOSQUE. IZNIK, MIDDLE OF THE 16TH CENTURY.
TOPKAPU SARAYI MUSEUM, ISTANBUL.

PORTRAIT OF SULTAN SELIM II (1566-1574) SHOOTING AN ARROW, WITH A PAGE ATTENDING HIM. BY REIS HAYDAR, CALLED NIGARI (1494-1572).
PORTRAIT GALLERY, TOPKAPU SARAYI MUSEUM, ISTANBUL.

Turkish portraiture at its best could satisfy many of the challenges posed by this demanding art. That a person's whole personality was well rendered is apparent when one looks at Nigari's portrait of Süleyman I with this statement by Busbeck in mind: "the sultan's forehead was hardly merry, his expression mournful but he showed sternness full of majesty." On the other hand, the portraitist's usual endeavor to present the sitter at his handsomest is demonstrated when Nigari's "Selim II" is considered together with Busbeck's reference to "Big Belly's mighty paunch, swollen cheeks and a face disfigured by a too-marked redness." Finally, Busbeck's description of a court reception shows how the setting in the paintings helped to create an ambiance which reflected the sitter's world; more specifically, it explains the motionless stance of the pages behind Süleyman and of the prince next to Ahmed III:

"More than anything else the silence and modesty of the large gathering deserved praise. One did not hear any voices or murmuring as one does in other places with such a strange medley of people; nor was there any rushing back or forth. In complete silence everybody kept the place due to his position... The several thousand janissaries offered an especially dignified spectacle as they stood separate from the rest in long rows and so motionless that, they being very far from me, I was for long uncertain whether they were men or statues."

Naturally, the same attitude of "attention" appears in many Turkish paintings of court receptions. While this strict demeanor gives these scenes, spectacular and colorful as they are, a rather wooden appearance, their immobility reflects nevertheless a typical aspect of official life and is as such an Ottoman style feature.

PORTRAIT OF SULTAN MEHMET II THE CONQUEROR (1451-1481). BY SINAN BEY.
PORTRAIT GALLERY, TOPKAPU SARAYI MUSEUM, ISTANBUL.

PORTRAIT OF SULTAN AHMED III (1703-1730) WITH PRINCE, BY LEVNI.
PORTRAIT GALLERY, TOPKAPU SARAYI MUSEUM, ISTANBUL.

In returning once more to Ottoman architecture after this brief survey of the tile production and the closely related manufacture of pottery, a word should be said about the second wall-in palace compound started by Mehmet the Conqueror, nowadays called "Topkapu" after a nearby cannon gate. All the structures now visible there in a succession of four courtyards are later. The kitchens designed by the great Sinan which now house the vast collections of Chinese porcelains are of the sixteenth century, while the council and audience chambers, as well as the kiosks, are of the seventeenth and eighteenth centuries or were at least rebuilt and decorated at that time. Other secular structures in a specific Ottoman style are caravanserais, bazaars, and public fountains—the latter either in the form of free-standing screened kiosks or of the simpler but still ornate wall-types. All these taken together with the large and small mosques and their dependencies, the *medreses*, *tekkes*, hospitals, libraries and *türbes* give the old Ottoman towns, especially Constantinople, their characteristic aspect.

With the advent of the industrial age and its mechanized traffic and the arrival of hordes of foreign tourists it would, however, be difficult to imagine what life in these ancient settings was like were it not for the pictorial records of former travelers. As Turkey and especially Constantinople have always exerted a great fascination on the West, we are fortunate in having a large series of views of towns and buildings, scenes of public and private life, and pictures of the specific garments worn by Turkish court officials, soldiers, traders and artisans as well as by the various minorities, both men and women. An early and most famous recorder of life in Turkey was Gentile Bellini who on invitation of Mehmet the Conqueror arrived in Constantinople in 1479 and stayed fifteen months during which time he painted his celebrated portrait of the sultan, now in the National Gallery, London, and also sculptured a portrait medal of him.

A very productive artist working during the reign of Süleyman the Magnificent was Melchior Lorichs of Flensburg, a follower of Albrecht Dürer, who accompanied Van Busbeck in 1555 on his embassy to Turkey and stayed on there for three and a half years; later, from 1570 to 1583, he worked on a large Turkish series of portraits, figure studies and views of buildings based on his Turkish observations, which was eventually published in 1626. Another very active painter of "turqueries" of a later age was the Frenchman Jean-Baptiste Vanmour, born in Valenciennes in 1671, who accompanied the French ambassador, the Marquis de Ferriol, to the Sublime Porte in 1699 and remained in the Turkish capital till his death in 1737. His many pictures and those of his school show every aspect of Turkish life, from the official to the intimate; included are topographical views, historical pictures and even scenes of the imperial harem and religious devotions.

Our knowledge of Turkish life is, however, not solely dependent on Western representations. Indeed there exists a body of Turkish paintings which, though still insufficiently explored, represents even as it stands today an invaluable source of detailed information. There are first the portraits of the sultans. The existing, quite sizable series is distinguished for the varied handling of the subject matter and for the psychological insights that are provided. This achievement is all the more remarkable as portrait painting was a novel task within the Muslim world where figural painting was officially forbidden. Yet the Ottoman painters achieved a long and diversified range of imperial likenesses, matched only by those of the Mughal Emperors of India, most of which, however, show us only the five or six outstanding members of the dynasty. Notwithstanding the fact that historical handbooks of the period of Murad III (1574-1595) begin to provide imaginary portraits of Ottoman rulers from the time of the earliest sultans, Osman and Orhan, the first painting which has the earmarks of an observed likeness is the *Portrait of Mehmet the Conqueror* by Sinan Bey. Sinan had studied in Venice and one may therefore assume that he owed to Italian influence the very idea of portraiture itself as well as the method of imparting corporeal substance by shading the face and the folds of the garments. However, his painting has Turkish aspects also which go well beyond the mere dress and posture and the traditional gesture of smelling a rose. The artist has converted the common Italian bust portrait (which was, for instance, used for Bellini's painting of the Conqueror) into a rendering of the whole figure, a not quite successful undertaking, as the crossed legs and feet are not properly indicated. He also stresses the corpulence of the body and sets it in sharp contrast to the strong-boned face, thereby underlining the sitter's physical strength and thoughtful determination. The sense of power is further stressed by the use of a few strong colors which occur in both the garments and the head and its covering. In spite of the flaws of the painting (which have been correctly assessed by the Turkish scholar Oktay Aslanapa) it has a definite monumental quality and it brings out even better than Bellini's likeness both the vigorous determination and the intellectual brilliance of the sitter. This portrait is a true blend of East and West and as such a fitting monument to this sultan and his aspirations.

The *Portrait of Sultan Süleyman the Magnificent in Old Age* by the painter Haydar Reis, called Nigari, presents an entirely different aspect. It has no Italianate quality; on the contrary, in the flat, unshaded handling of figures and colors the artist has returned to the main stream of Near Eastern painting. Our first sensation comes here from the unusual black background which brings out the brilliant colors of the garments (especially those of the two court pages) but imparts also a somber note to the whole. The second impression is that of the austere simplicity of the sultan himself, whose immense turban above a thin, grey face gives him nevertheless the appearance of authority. Although the minute floral symbol in the lower right corner and the position of the legs imply a walk in a garden, his figure seems motionless; only the slightly lifted left hand gives an indication of inner life. This is however not discernible in the two pages who follow a few steps behind their master. Their immobile position, compact grouping, and frozen expressions all underline the awe-inspiring majesty of the ruler in his slow, silent walk.

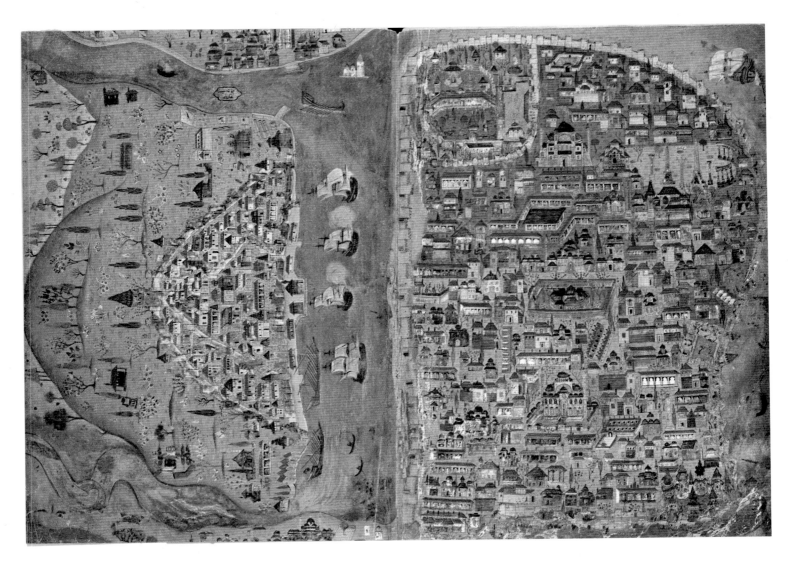

VIEW OF CONSTANTINOPLE AND GALATA. FROM NASUH AS-SILAHI AL-MATRAKI'S "DESCRIPTION OF THE STAGES OF SULTAN SÜLEYMAN'S CAMPAIGN IN THE TWO IRAQS." 1537. UNIVERSITY LIBRARY, ISTANBUL.

The same painter's *Portrait of Selim II* is handled in an entirely different fashion and is the first to show the figure in action. As his highly lifted arm indicates, the sultan has just dispatched an arrow toward a target held by a retainer in the right section of the double composition and now appears to be expectantly watching its course. Along with these signs of physical and mental activity another feature attracts our attention: the display of refined luxury shown by the richly patterned garments of all the figures as well as by the long, elegant curls of the foppishly dressed page behind the sultan. Although Selim's person does not reveal the special qualities of his illustrious father and ancestor—which indeed he did not have—he still appears here by dint of size, action, and splendor as an imposing figure fully capable of focusing our interest.

The contrast of these three portraits of the classical period to one created during the late flowering of Ottoman art is striking. The painting by Levni, one of the last great court artists, of *Ahmed III (1703-1730) and his Son* has turned into one of mere display. The imposing garments and turbans, the elaborate flower-decorated throne and carpet are all meant to reveal the wealth and splendor of the "Shadow of God on Earth." By contrast, the human interest in the inner qualities of the father's personality is lost, as the artist has endeavored to present a formal state portrait in which the more intimate features of this pleasure-loving and poetic sultan are suppressed. He appears only as a stern autocrat in whose presence even a prince must stand in respectful silence.

The portraits of the sultans represent, however, only one aspect of Ottoman painting. Manuscript illustrations seem to have been first executed under Bayazid II, as a copy of Shaikhi's *Khosrow and Shirin* of 1499 in the Uppsala University Library indicates. Although this volume betrays the impact of Persian miniature painting of the School of Herat and also some slight western influence, a specific Turkish manner can already be noticed in a greater spatial clarity and a tendency to simplify figures, architecture

VIEW OF SULTANIYE (TABRIZ) WITH THE MAUSOLEUM OF OLJEITU KHUDABANDEH. FROM NASUH AS-SILAHI AL-MATRAKI'S "DESCRIPTION OF THE STAGES OF SULTAN SÜLEYMAN'S CAMPAIGN IN THE TWO IRAQS." 1537. UNIVERSITY LIBRARY, ISTANBUL.

and landscape. One of the earliest illustrated manuscripts preserved in Istanbul to-day is a copy of Nasuh as-Silahi al-Matraki's *Description of the Stages of Sultan Süleyman's Campaign in the Two Iraqs* (that is, Arab and Persian) of 1537 in the University Library. In depicting the towns through which the sultan had passed or the sites where he pitched his camps, the writer-painter used an illustrative system which is halfway between the objectivity of a map and the decorative splendor of a miniature. While al-Matraki is specific in his delineation of the topographical character of a site and particularly careful in portraying the main buildings—rendering all this as seen from a high vantage point—he does not hesitate to use conventional though always delightful symbols to indicate secondary features such as simple houses, fortifications, vegetation, rivers, bridges, and mountains. He was, however, unwilling to include human figures which might have enlivened the scenes although he occasionally shows animals or ships. Since everything is given in the bright, cheerful colors and simple alignment of little toy towns with all signs of poverty or human labor omitted, these paintings have a naive charm and gaiety all their own. Yet they are also valuable documents since many of the famous buildings have disappeared or are today in a sadly ruined state. One thinks, for example, of the magnificent, richly decorated mausoleum of the Mongol ruler Oljeitu Khudabandeh of 1313 in Sultaniye in North-west Persia whose still well-preserved structure in its complete setting appears in a delightful two-page composition.

The great period of figural miniature painting falls in the reign of Sultan Murad III (1574-1595). Unlike the polychrome paintings of Iran which nearly always deal with a heroic or romantic aspect of the nation's remote past, the Turkish painters were to a large extent concerned with the contemporary or near-contemporary achievements of the house of Osman. For the treatment of such subjects they still used the basic conventions developed by Persian miniaturists such as the high vantage point, the placing of the main scene in the middle ground or slightly behind it against an archi-tectural or landscape backdrop, and the flat treatment of small puppet-like figures; however, they imbue such settings and actors with an entirely different spirit of realism. In the two preserved volumes (originally four) of the *Book of Accomplishments (Hüner-nameh)* by al-Ashuri of 1579-1584 in the Topkapu Sarayı Museum, the court artist Osman and his school portrayed Ottoman history down to the period of Süleyman, giving the closest attention to garments, turbans, uniforms, and weapons as well as to the topographic *mise en scène*. In the peacetime subjects the composition is usually controlled by the ordered arrangement of the courtiers in front and to the sides of the large-size figure of the sultan; by contrast, the war episodes show primarily the invincible Turkish army advancing in a kind of steamroller effect with its compact rows of riflebearing janissaries and cannon brigades under the command of the sultan or pasha. However valuable such accurate documentation may be, the artistic presen-tation often suffered from it, as it led to stiffly arranged figures, standing according to strict protocol, or to the serried alignment of row upon row of soldiers.

MARY AND JESUS IN A LANDSCAPE. MINIATURE IN A "BOOK OF FORTUNE TELLING" COMPOSED FOR SULTAN AHMED I BY QALENDER. EARLY 17TH CENTURY. FOLIO 32 RECTO, HAZINE 1703, TOPKAPU SARAYI LIBRARY, ISTANBUL.

EZEKIEL RAISING THE DEAD. MINIATURE FROM LUQMAN,
SON OF HUSEYN AL-ASHURI OF URMIYA'S "CREAM OF HISTORIES" WRITTEN IN 1583.
FOLIO 35a (DETAIL), NO. 1973, MUSEUM OF TURKISH AND ISLAMIC ART, ISTANBUL.

A second type of manuscript illustration developed during Murad III's reign avoided these problems. This occurs in the *Book of the Festival (Sur-nameh)* whose miniatures depict the forty-day celebrations on the occasion of the circumcision of the sultan's son; they show in particular the parades of tradespeople, artisans and entertainers in front of the grandstand with the boxes of the sultan, his court and the European ambassadors. While this illustrious audience in the back remains about the same throughout the manuscript, the main scenes of the foreground, which represents the old hippodrome of Constantinople, vary from miniature to miniature as they show the many guilds with their different symbols of trade or small movable versions of their workshops. The candid and often droll portrayal of the middle and lower classes represents the real artistic and sociological interest of these paintings; it established a whole new genre which lasted till about 1720-1725 when under Ahmed III a similar *Sur-nameh* was written and illustrated by Levni and his school. Besides these two major efforts there are other paintings where the ordinary people of the city are portrayed, often with a keen sense of humor and the use of caricature.

A third type of painting is also typically Turkish and it, too, led to a special artistic expression. These are the illustrations of sacred history. They may be accounts of a Biblical nature, as Old and New Testament stories were told or alluded to in the Koran and therefore belong to the Islamic imagery, or they may deal with the time and life of the Prophet Muhammad and the early believers. In certain instances they form the prelude of later Ottoman dynastic history while in others they constitute a distinct genre of their own. In either case they are unusually far ranging and form altogether a remarkable set of pictures within a civilization which was strictly orthodox and therefore in its general artistic production (especially in the decorative arts) adverse to figural images. Many of these Turkish paintings—like the forty miniatures in the *Cream of Histories (Zübdet at-tevarih)* of 1583 in the Museum of Turkish and Islamic Art in Istanbul—have a monumental quality and often even a largeness of scale—real or implied—which sets them apart not only from most of the other Ottoman paintings but even more markedly from the pictorial arts of Iran and India. Their interest is fully concentrated on the main action or on a specific figure, paying little attention to beautiful though distracting details of the architectural or landscape setting or to elaborate patterns of garments. These miniatures may perhaps have a stark, unbending quality which formerly might have repelled connoisseurs accustomed to the lyric charm and decorative quality of fifteenth- and sixteenth-century Persian painting but which in its uncompromising, at times even shocking directness is greatly appealing to the modern mind.

As can be imagined from the realistic aspect of Ottoman paintings, they are important documents for the political, military, and social history of Turkey. They also furnish important clues for certain artistic details. Thus, while many miniatures show the kaftans or outer robes worn by various personages to be plain-colored or decorated with hardly recognizable patterns, some are more explicit, depicting not only the kaftans of the sultan, but other decorated textiles as well—either spread on the ground for the proper reception of the mounted ruler, placed on a barrier to hold back the crowds during an imperial entry, or carried by artisans in the great parades. Yet even these representations, though they give an indication of the patterns used, are really too small to convey any adequate idea of the innate beauty of these silks and velvets. For the full aesthetic impression we must turn to actual pieces of the fabrics; when securely documented and viewed in the light of information culled from archives, these can also help us to an understanding of the historical development.

KAFTAN OF MURAD IV (1623-1640). COSTUME GALLERY, TOPKAPU SARAYI MUSEUM, ISTANBUL.

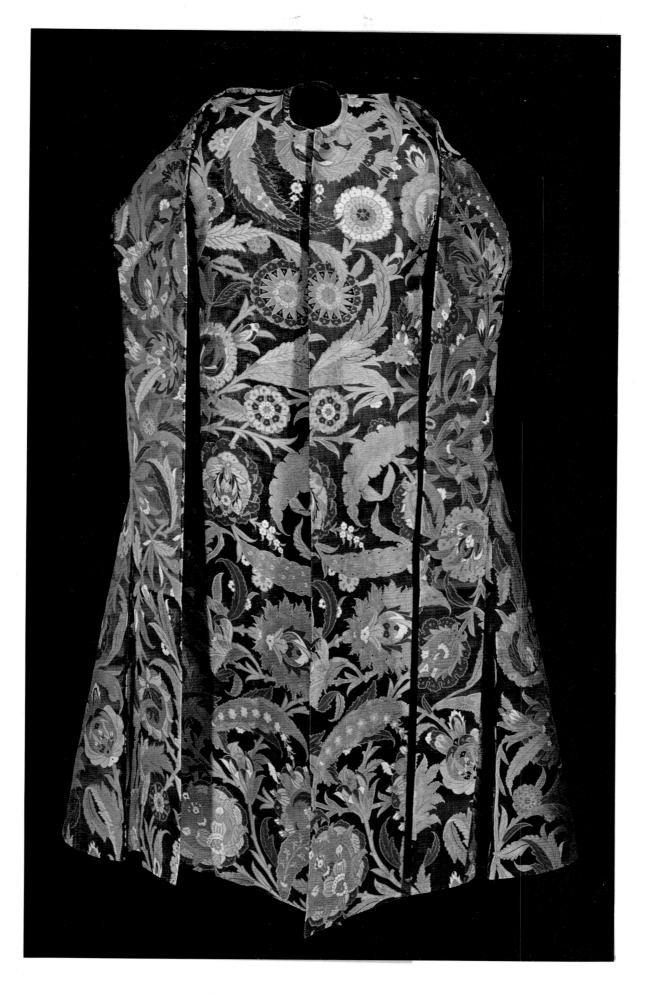

KAFTAN OF BAYAZID II (1481-1512). COSTUME GALLERY, TOPKAPU SARAYI MUSEUM, ISTANBUL.

We thus learn that textiles, including figured fabrics, were produced in several places, as early as the time of Osman I at the end of the thirteenth century, and that this production apparently increased in the fourteenth. This indicates that an industry which had started under the Seljuks (see above p. 159) continued to flourish under the Ottomans. The earliest preserved piece with proper documentation is a gold brocaded variegated silk of an unusual pattern consisting of stripes with alternating floral or geometric designs and inscriptions. One of these mentions a "Sultan Bayazid Khan" who for historical and stylistic reasons must be the first Ottoman ruler of that name, called Yildirim, "the Thunderer." This important fabric apparently served as the cover of a coffin or sarcophagus and is now in the Treasury of the Monastery of Studenica in Yugoslavia which in the late fourteenth century was in the sphere of Ottoman influence. Beginning with Mehmet the Conqueror ample material exists, for the opening of the ancient palaces showed that from that period till practically the end of the sultanate the authorities preserved the garments of the deceased rulers, members of their families and even of small children, all well wrapped and labelled. In addition the archives give us further information about the character of the robes, their patterns, techniques and weights, the heads of the workshops and their staffs, and the imperial efforts to preserve the high quality of the production; they teach us in particular that in the fifteenth century the production center was Bursa and that after its conquest Istanbul, too, played a major role, with Mardin, Amasya, Damascus, Baghdad, and Chios making important contributions. The results of this wide-spread, well-organized industry are amazing and it is particularly significant that the artistic level of the silks and velvets remained high till the eighteenth century—even at a time, that is, when the quality of the products in other media had greatly declined.

A selection of choice pieces in a special Costume Gallery in the Topkapu Sarayı Museum gives an inkling of the outstanding artistic quality and great variety of these robes, many of them enriched with gold and silver threads. In this account only a mere sampling must suffice. A kaftan of Bayazid II of gold brocaded velvet presents a riotous arrangement of Hatayi flowers on a deep brown ground against which the reds and greens, the yellow and white shine all the more brightly. Although there is only a limited number of such flowers in addition to the lanceolated leaves, the movement of their composition, their changing colors, and the application of one pattern upon another makes this a splendid garment. It is remarkable how varied the floral motifs in these garments are. Thus the kaftans of the period of Mehmet the Conqueror use very large-scale yellow pomegranate or artichoke patterns framed on each side by a crescent-shaped serrated leaf of which two sets on a white ground are sufficient for each side of the robe. On the other hand the garments of the middle and later sixteenth century use the then popular flowers—tulips foremost among them—either in strict arrangements such as ogival compartments or in free-flowing alignments. Only in the eighteenth century do the floral units lose their impressive large format and turn into small units eventually arranged in rows. In the time of Süleyman the Magnificent formal

HELMET INLAID WITH GOLD AND ENCRUSTED WITH RUBIES AND TURQUOISES. 16TH CENTURY.
TREASURY OF THE TOPKAPU SARAYI MUSEUM, ISTANBUL.

IVORY MIRROR WITH EBONY HANDLE MADE FOR SULTAN SÜLEYMAN THE MAGNIFICENT (1520-1566)
AND CARVED BY GHANI IN 1543. COSTUME GALLERY, TOPKAPU SARAYI MUSEUM, ISTANBUL.

designs became a more frequent part of the weaver's repertory and one finds for
instance the various symbols of celestial bodies, especially the crescent moon which at
that time, however, had neither the political nor religious significance that it acquired
in the early nineteenth century. Another popular device which had already occurred
on a robe of Mehmet the Conqueror was the "three ball motif"; this was often combined
with two wavy tiger stripes (or cloudlike bands), a typical Ottoman pattern not yet
satisfactorily explained. A kaftan of Murad IV (1623-1640) which presents these two
patterns in the typical Ottoman color combination of gold on red, shows that in the
seventeenth century the weavers could still produce bold designs which made magnificent robes. In view of such outstanding aesthetic qualities, it is easy to understand that
Turkish textiles from the fifteenth century to the eighteenth had a wide influence.
When Selim I defeated the Iranians his booty from the Persian capital included Turkish
textiles. The West was no less eager to own these precious fabrics, which were exported
to Europe as far as Sweden. They even influenced textile production in other regions,
particularly in Italy whose orientalizing versions of the imported fabrics influenced

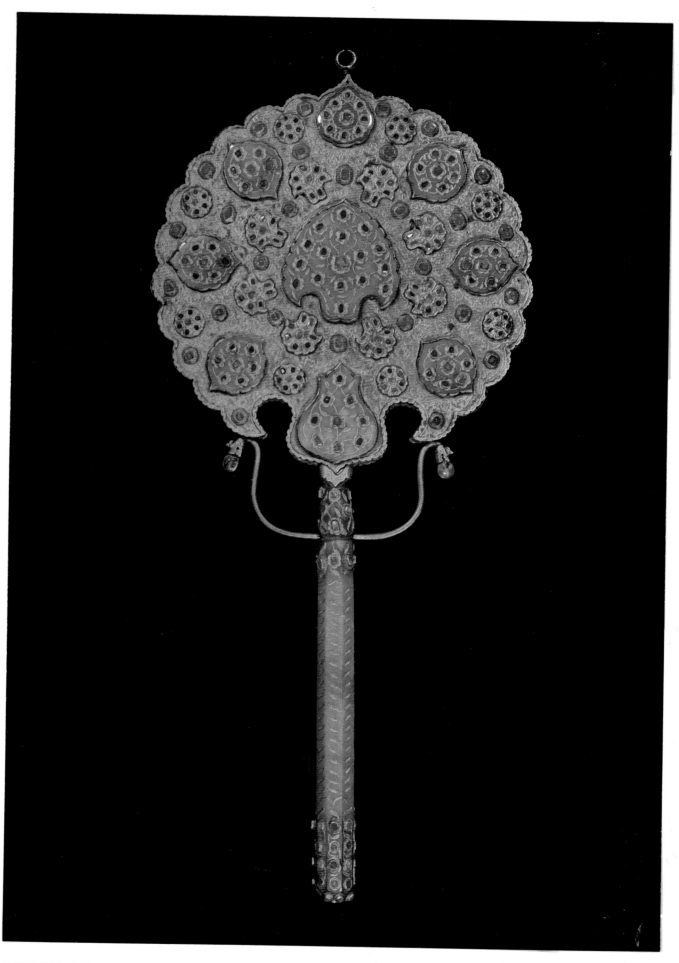

MIRROR DECORATED WITH JADE MEDALLIONS INLAID WITH GOLD AND ENCRUSTED WITH RUBIES AND EMERALDS. 16TH-17TH CENTURY.
TREASURY OF THE TOPKAPU SARAYI MUSEUM, ISTANBUL.

THRONE OF SULTAN AHMED I (1603-1617), MADE OF WALNUT,
INLAID WITH MOTHER-OF-PEARL AND TORTOISE-SHELL AND ENCRUSTED WITH PRECIOUS STONES.
TREASURY OF THE TOPKAPU SARAYI MUSEUM, ISTANBUL.

Ottoman textiles in turn. The woven patterns were also copied as embroideries not only in the homes of Anatolia and European Turkey but also in the Greek islands and as far west as Algiers and Tetuan.

Just as the brilliant robes of the sultans symbolized their peacetime power and splendor so did their arms and armor proclaim their prowess in war. The helmets and body armor of the fifteenth century are boldly conceived and show strong, robust forms whose steel surfaces are decorated with large-scale floral patterns and big inscriptions inlaid in silver or occasionally in gold. In the sixteenth century the helmets became more attenuated and cloche-like and thus assume a more elegant shape. Inscriptions still play an important role, as they plead for divine succour by means of appropriate passages from the Koran or invocations of Muslim saints. In addition, a delicate floral decoration now appears which, like the inscriptions, is often inlaid in gold. For parade purposes these pieces were even studded with rubies, garnets, and turquoises, but even so the jewelled decoration applied to helmets, swords, and daggers did not interfere with their original function. With their splendid ornaments they served both as military equipment and as symbols of a warrior's high station and are therefore appropriately found today in armories and art museums alike.

The jewelled weapons of the Ottomans lead us to their *arts somptuaires*. Most of this luxury production was connected with the person of the sultan. The Treasury of the Topkapu Sarayı Museum thus contains a number of thrones, of which the high seat and baldachin of Ahmed I is one of the most spectacular. Its wooden base presents another type of inlay characteristic for Ottoman work which employs applications of mother-of-pearl, tortoise-shell, and precious stones. They form here floral patterns, with the ever-popular tulips and carnations either emanating realistically from vases or shaped into conventionalized floral scrolls. A special feature of these thrones is a large jewelled arrangement in a golden mounting which was suspended directly above the head of the ruler and apparently served to symbolize his supernatural splendor. The Treasury of the former Palace still boasts several examples of these deliberately showy ornaments, each in a different arrangement of the precious materials. A functional implement that received a sumptuous housing was the mirror for imperial use. The mirror once owned by Süleyman the Magnificent is delicately carved from an ivory plaque the back of which is densely covered with all the favorite decorative patterns popular at this time: arabesques, floral rosettes, cloud bands, and finally, along the scalloped edge, an intricately written inscription on a floral background which includes the names of the sultan and the carver, Ghani, as well as the date, 1543. A less delicate but much more spectacular creation is a slightly later mirror in which the goldsmith's work is combined with inlaid jade pieces, and a rich display of rubies and emeralds is applied to both the jade handle and the fanlike reverse. The application of precious or semi-precious stones became a Turkish specialty and we find them not only on the more usual objects of personal use and weapons but also on book bindings and even applied to Chinese porcelains.

PRAYER RUG SAID TO HAVE BELONGED TO SULTAN AHMED I (1603-1617).
KNOTTED IN CAIRO, EARLY 17TH CENTURY. TOPKAPU SARAYI MUSEUM, ISTANBUL.

KNOTTED WOOLLEN CARPET OF THE TYPE CALLED "LARGE-PATTERNED HOLBEIN RUG."
BERGAMA DISTRICT, 16TH CENTURY. MUSEUM OF TURKISH AND ISLAMIC ART, ISTANBUL.

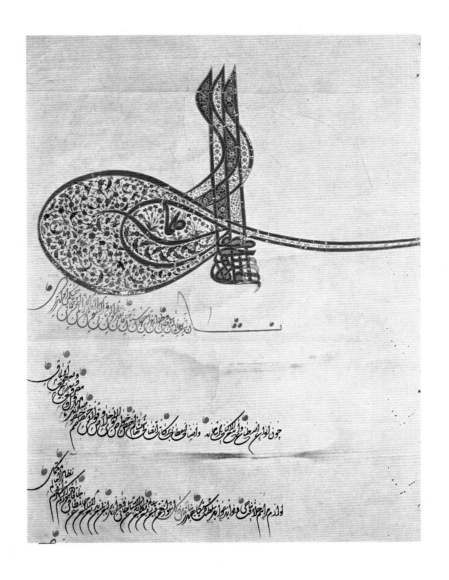

IMPERIAL EDICT (FERMAN) TOPPED BY THE IMPERIAL CALLIGRAPHIC EMBLEM (TUGHRA)
OF SULTAN SÜLEYMAN THE MAGNIFICENT (1520-1566),
DETAIL. 1556. NO. 2231, MUSEUM OF TURKISH AND ISLAMIC ART, ISTANBUL.

In contrast to the court pieces just described, there existed a production which never
lost its folk character though the great demand that eventually greeted its output
brought about a highly organized semi-industrial system of manufacture. We are
referring to the carpets of Anatolia, the earliest of which, as we have already seen, date
from the thirteenth century. Departing from fourteenth-century usage which continued
into the fifteenth, the newly evolving types that crystallized in the course of the latter
century deleted nearly every form of animal design and replaced it by geometric
patterns which in certain cases were combined with highly stylized floral forms. In this
period three major basic types were developed. Two of these show the same underlying
scheme of staggered rows of diamond- and octagon-shaped units but differ so completely in their detailed execution and coloring that their close compositional relationship
has only recently been recognized.

The first type has long been designated as "the small-patterned Holbein carpets" while the second is nowadays associated with Lorenzo Lotto—the name deriving in each case from characteristic representations of such carpets in paintings of these masters. Only the third variety has a close connection with the previously popular animal carpets inasmuch as it is also composed of a series of squares into which octagons filled with other designs are inserted. These are aligned in a single longitudinal row (or—again as seen in paintings—in double rows) in which the units are separated from one another and from the border by ornamental stripes. This type came into being in the fifteenth century, as we know from paintings by Jan van Eyck, while later examples are to be found accurately delineated in the pictures of Memling, Ghirlandaio, and particularly in those of Holbein the Younger, after whom they are usually called "the large-patterned Holbein carpets." Their ground is usually red (as in many textiles), although a strong brown occurs also, while the filling motifs of stars or rosettes in the octagons show a variety of colors which give each unit a somewhat kaleidoscopic look. In some slightly later examples two small-scale octagons are placed above and below the large units— a form of compositional subordination which replaces the earlier generally used system of coordination and was probably due to the influence of fifteenth-century carpets from Egypt. Unlike the two other types of carpets developed in the fifteenth century, this one continued in the Bergama region practically until our own times and it is therefore assumed that its pattern was originally developed there. The type was copied as early as the fifteenth century in Spain where even the arrangement of two latitudinal rows of octagons in squares occurs, although no originals from the Near East have survived. In the eighteenth and nineteenth century the compositional scheme also became known in the Caucasus and was then copied in a reduced fashion in the so-called "Kazaks" and in the "Soumak kilims."

The folk quality of all these Turkish carpets and others produced in Anatolia is evident from the long persistence of fairly fixed patterns, their basically simple but bold character and the strong colors used; another factor is the rather coarse appearance and hard drawing of the designs resulting from the employment of the "Turkish or Gördes knot," in which the yarns are securely twisted around two warp threads. Manifestly, this sturdy production was not quite in keeping with the aesthetic refinement and technical excellence of other arts, especially the textile and pottery production. Two events changed this. In 1514 Selim I conquered Tabriz, temporarily at least, and three years later also Cairo, which like the whole of Egypt remained for centuries in Ottoman hands. Both capitals had flourishing carpet manufactures whose different artistic principles, color scheme, and technique were now combined with Turkish designs for the creation of a new courtly type of carpet. It is nowadays assumed that in the second or third decade of the sixteenth century, model designs were dispatched to Egypt from a still unknown center, probably Constantinople, to be executed in the established Cairene workshops. These designs were based on the Northwest Persian composition scheme of a central medallion, now usually round and small, and quarter medallions in the four corners of the field which was otherwise filled with the usual vegetal patterns of rosette and palmette flowers, curved lanceolate leaves and arabesques, and later on with even more pronouncedly Ottoman motifs such as the double-cloud bands, tulips, carnations, hyacinths, and other "Turkish blossoms." These ground filling designs took on a specially rich and lush appearance of nearly Baroque character which is perhaps even more luxuriant than the contemporary textile and tile patterns. For these carpets the "Persian or Senna knot" long customary in Cairo was used, which allowed a greater fineness of design than the "Turkish knot"; the lustrous silky wool of the earlier Egyptian production continued to form the raw material, and at first even the old color scheme was adhered to. The latter was then extended to a richer palette amongst whose seven to eight tones a deep red, light blue, green, yellow and white predominated. In the final treatment of the field and borders during the best period, which lasted from the middle of the sixteenth century for about a century, these characteristically Turkish carpets formed one of the finest carpet

CALLIGRAPHIC DESIGN OF THE ARABIC PHRASE "PRAISE TO THE SAINT, PRAISE!" BY AHMED QARA-HISARI. 16TH CENTURY. NO. 1443, MUSEUM OF TURKISH AND ISLAMIC ART, ISTANBUL.

categories produced in the Near East. They exist in the usual rectangular format, sometimes of a very large size, but there are also square and round examples and even a cross-shaped variety. An especially attractive group of the early seventeenth century is the prayer rugs in which the central red or green niche-shaped field may be empty, although in the finest pieces this area, like the border, is filled with gay flower and leaf arrangements while the spandrels are decorated with delicately drawn arabesques. These carpets display an elegance of design and a warm satisfying range of colors which make them one of the most successful creations of the Golden Age of Ottoman art.

At the end of this discussion a word should be said about one more artistic endeavor, calligraphic writing. Calligraphy exists in its own right but is also to be found century after century in one way or another as a decorative feature in all the various media, whether for sacred or secular use. It is, of course, the Islamic art par excellence and Turkey therefore shares many of the standard scripts with other Muslim countries of the Near East. A case in point is the *sulus* script which was very popular not only in Egypt but in Turkey as well and was applied there to buildings and cenotaphs, employed for chapter headings, and used in all places where a large-scale, well-proportioned inscription was appropriate. But the Ottomans also developed scripts which are entirely their own, among which one called *riqʻa* was the most widely used for manuscripts, letters, and even later on for printing types. The Muslim connoisseurs of other countries have somewhat condescendingly looked down on Ottoman calligraphers, as is for instance evident from the opinion expressed by the Persian writer on calligraphy Qadi Ahmed who, in about 1606, had this to say of a certain practitioner: "Mūsā-Bey, although a Turk by origin, was a possessor of accomplishments and wrote excellently in the *nastaʻliq* style." Actually the Turks have produced some remarkable hands, though primarily in the more sturdy and monumental varieties, and their pronounced aptitude lasted till the days when the Arabic alphabet was officially changed for the Latin one in 1928. One of the great masters was Ahmed Qara-Hisari who worked in the period of Selim I and Süleyman the Magnificent and who designed a special inscription for Süleyman's mosque. He was proficient in many hands and an album in the Museum for Turkish and Islamic Art in Istanbul gives ample proof of his calligraphic versatility and finesse, even in such an unusual type of writing as square Kufic. What is especially noteworthy in his œuvre is his endeavor to create novel rhythmic patterns by the condensing, stretching and looping of letters without, however, sacrificing any of their clarity of character. The same tendency can also be observed in another deliberately rhythmic script developed for official chancellery use called *diwani*, employed in gold, blue, and black inks for the imperial diplomas and *fermans* or edicts. These were always preceded by the *tughra*, originally meaning a seal or a sign, and specifically standing for the large, monogram-like rendition of the sultan's name given in lieu of his signature to make the document legally binding. A typical example of these two characteristic varieties of Ottoman calligraphy is to be found in an edict of 1556 issued by Süleyman the Magnificent.

CALLIGRAPHIC FOURFOLD DESIGN BASED ON THE MULTIPLE APPLICATION OF THE NAME ALI IN SQUARE KUFIC WRITING.
PROBABLY FROM CENTRAL ASIA, 15TH CENTURY. FOLIO 9 VERSO, HAZINE 2152, TOPKAPU SARAYI LIBRARY, ISTANBUL.

THE TREASURES OF THE SULTANS

It would be wrong to assume that the art objects found in Turkey reflect only the long and illustrious past of the country. Istanbul, once the capital of a vast empire, holds a position similar to that of London, Paris, or the Vatican in that its art collections mirror its world-wide connections and present a universal aspect. The existence of spectacular pieces from many countries may be due to various causes: many reached the capital as booty, others as royal presents; another category, again, came through trade while still another important group of more recent date is the result of excavations conducted in various parts of the former empire. The contents of the Museum of Oriental Antiquities, the Archaeological Museum, and the Topkapu Sarayı Museum and its Library give ample evidence of these historical processes. As a result, the histories of Sumerian, Babylonian, and Assyrian antiquities cannot be written without making constant reference to the collections in Istanbul and the same applies to such an entirely different subject as Chinese porcelains of the fourteenth to the seventeenth century. While most of the visitors to Istanbul are made aware of this fact through the many public displays, other splendid treasures stored in various depositories are more likely to remain unknown to them. To these belong, for instance, the holdings in the Library of manuscripts connected with various sultans. Thus the account of *Arab Painting*, which was recently published in the series *Treasures of Asia*, could not have been written without the many hitherto unknown documents in the library of Ahmed III, the same sultan whose portrait by Levni was discussed in the previous chapter. There are, furthermore, thousands of exquisite Persian miniatures waiting to be unearthed, and, to judge from previous discoveries, their eventual publication will greatly change our understanding of the development of this art. Even less known are the Chinese, Central Asian, and Indian paintings, drawings, and documents deposited on various library shelves. All we can do at this point is to present some samples of the unusual, but greatly appealing, treasures which reached Istanbul in one way or another.

There are a number of albums in the Treasury of the Topkapu Sarayı Museum which were part of the booty of Selim I after his victory over the Persians in the battle of Chaldiran in 1514. They contain an enormous number of paintings and calligraphic specimens by some of the most illustrious masters of the fourteenth and fifteenth centuries and are thus often connected with the best-known royal patrons of the arts of that period. In many cases, furthermore, they are the only remaining survivors of whole schools of art. Among them is a composition which stands halfway between calligraphy and abstract painting. In its general composition it resembles square Kufic compositions of the type found in the pen exercises of Ahmed Qara-Hisari and like these goes back to earlier prototypes which had probably been inspired by Chinese seal characters. But while these sixteenth-century examples can be read with some endeavor, the specimen in the album presents more of a problem. In cryptic fashion each quarter contains several times the name of Ali, the fourth caliph and main Shi'ite saint, repeated in various colors and different positions; the intricacy of the composition is increased by the fact that the letters consist of broken lines and dots which are made to cross each other. When put together the four parts form a swastika-like composition which in its complexity and coloristic appeal can easily compete with Mondrian. Square Kufic arrangements of the more usual type were made in Iran in the first half of the fourteenth century and in Turkestan later in that century and in the first half of the next; as nothing of this type has ever been found among the much better documented Iranian material, it seems more likely that this beautiful graphic riddle comes from Central Asia, for instance from Samarkand, where it could have been made in the early fifteenth century.

An entirely different world is opened by a large series of figural drawings which are all interrelated but fall easily in two major groups, if we except a long scroll painting of wild animals, chiefly jackals and fierce dogs, which in spirit and style, however, belongs to the first category. This first group shows black-, red- or yellow-skinned demons with fearsome horned heads whose wrinkled faces are endowed with fiery eyes and large teeth protruding from broad, leering mouths. These heads have hardly any neck to connect them with their stocky bodies which are distinguished by rows of heavy legs ending in broad-toed, clawed feet and, at times, long animal tails. The weird creatures wear only a loincloth, though some boast metal rings around the short necks, arms, wrists and ankles. Their activities or attitudes are of a truly demoniac nature. They are often involved in fierce fights with one another, they subdue dragons, carry off great horses as easily as if they were lambs, thereby indicating their huge size, or grasp large, bloody hunks of animal flesh; indeed they are so violent that many are shown fettered by chains with horsewhips near at hand. Only occasionally do they present less brutish aspects, as when they are depicted making music, dancing wildly with twisted scarves, drinking from fine Chinese porcelain bottles, or carrying elaborate aerial sedan chairs in which beautiful Chinese princesses are seated. The hairiness of their bodies, indicative of their non-human nature, is brought out by a pointillistic painting technique or the application of many fine strokes, though solid washes also occur as they do throughout the second major group. In either case the colors are somber, with browns and grays predominating, and even when reds and blues are used they have a dull finish. In the scenes involving these demons as well as in the second group there is rarely an indication of a landscape; only an occasional rock, flower or tree trunk serving as a kind of stage property gives some indication of the setting. While the demons seem to be possessed by a wild fiendish spirit as if imbued with inner tension and a readiness to be instantly aroused, the figures of the other category move slowly and deliberately and at times appear to be asleep or lost in a trance. Most of them are men, though women and even children occur also. They are heavily clothed in thick, padded cloaks whose folds are much like those of their faces. They wear cloche-like hats while their feet are either bare or shod with heavy shoes. Their faces appear worn and they often stare at one another or into the infinite, this look being made even more pronounced by the lack of a pupil in the iris. These are obviously human figures and are thus engaged in the ordinary daily activities of the herdsman tending animals or the artisan engaged in carpentry or other work. Scenes of violence are not lacking however: in one case a man looks with bland bewilderment at a prostrate figure whom he has just felled with a big rock, while in another painting a fur-clad giant, apparently the hero of the tribe, is engaged in a mortal combat with one of the hostile demons, whom he has lifted in his arms and holds head downward as if about to hurl him violently to the ground. A third human group is again different: here the figures wear only a loincloth and neck scarf; their heads, too, are bare. They are engaged in meditation, quiet conversation, music-making, or in wild dances, perhaps of a ritualistic nature. These figures seem less fettered to the strain of a slow and down-trodden existence but reflect a more spiritual life and might be priests or shamans.

Since these paintings do not belong to any of the well-established Iranian, Central Asian, or Ottoman schools, there has naturally been some speculation as to the region and date to which they should be attributed. A certain indication is given by their style and technique. There are a good many Chinese elements in these paintings; even the general character and coloring are not too far removed from the Far Eastern world. Perhaps the most telling indication of this relationship is the occurrence of silk as the painting ground and the occasional arrangement of the figures into hand scrolls in the Chinese manner, though the personages are now divided into smaller units. These curious and unique paintings must therefore come from a region which was under stronger Chinese influence than that to be found in the Iranian and main Central Asian schools; this suggests a tribal area in Central Asia or another region marginal to China. An additional indication of the origin of these paintings is provided by their ancient attribution in Persian to an Ustad Muhammad Siyah-Qalam or "Master Muhammad Black Pen." Although the title as given and the often awkward placing of these inscriptions on the paintings of both groups precludes their being actual signatures of the artist, they not only provide a useful generic term for the whole category but, in spite of the commonness of the name, a clue to the painter. Professor Z.V. Togan of the University of Istanbul has identified him with a Muhammad Naqqash, active in the second half of the fifteenth century, who was said to be Herat's greatest painter and of whom it was stated that he "drew strange events and wonderful figures" and who after "much effort managed to make some pottery plates resembling Chinese porcelains." In this context it is therefore significant that large, well-drawn Chinese porcelain vessels occur occasionally in these colored drawings. It was also pointed out by the same Turkish scholar that some of the Timurid rulers who had a close connection with Herat stayed for long periods of time in the steppe country of Kho-rezm, Central Asia, and even western Siberia. All this tallies with the content, style,

TWO MEN IN A RITUAL DANCE. PAINTING DRAWN IN THE MANNER OF MUHAMMAD SIYAH-QALAM. MIDDLE TO SECOND HALF OF 15TH CENTURY. FOLIO 34 VERSO, HAZINE 2153, TOPKAPU SARAYI LIBRARY, ISTANBUL.

THREE OLD MEN. PAINTING ATTRIBUTED TO USTAD MUHAMMAD SIYAH-QALAM ("MASTER MUHAMMAD BLACK PEN").
MIDDLE TO SECOND HALF OF 15TH CENTURY. FOLIO 85 VERSO, HAZINE 2160, TOPKAPU SARAYI LIBRARY, ISTANBUL.

One is, of course, first impressed by the artistic quality and uniqueness of this whole group of paintings, which casts a real spell on the viewer. What makes them particularly important in the context of this book is the fact that they apparently constitute a vivid reflection of life among Turkic people of Central Asia when still unaffected by Islam. Indeed the only major religious document among them which does not deal with the tribal beliefs represents a Christian subject. The contrast to Persian painting is also significant: instead of colorful illustrations of books dealing with legendary heroic feats or amatory episodes in a courtly milieu, we encounter realistic pictures of the coloristically subdued world of demons and downtrodden tribesmen. Such emotional explorations of the violent forces of the supernatural world and of the humble doings of ordinary mortals were well beyond the usual interests of Iranian painters of that time. This is the first extensive visualization of the physical and spiritual aspects of another society and as such it is as significant in the intellectual history of the Middle East as al-Kindi's book of South Arabian antiquities in the ninth century, al-Biruni's account of India (c. 1030) or ash-Shahrastani's treatise on various philosophical and religious systems (1127). In their manner of presentation these painters were also innovators: their style combines the monumental qualities of the Iranian miniatures of the first half of the fourteenth century with the realism first encountered in marginal designs from the early fifteenth century but only in the second half of the sixteenth or early seventeenth century more widely directed to the lower classes and pastoral themes of Iran. By regarding the pictorial medium as a self-contained record and not as mere illustrations, these paintings are also way ahead of their time.

DEMON LEANING ON A STAFF. PAINTING ATTRIBUTED TO MUHAMMAD SIYAH-QALAM.
MIDDLE TO SECOND HALF OF 15TH CENTURY.
FOLIO 23a, HAZINE 2153, TOPKAPU SARAYI LIBRARY, ISTANBUL.

OLD MAN TENDING A HORSE. PAINTING ATTRIBUTED TO MUHAMMAD SIYAH-QALAM. MIDDLE TO SECOND HALF OF 15TH CENTURY. FOLIO 50 VERSO, HAZINE 2160, TOPKAPU SARAYI LIBRARY, ISTANBUL.

LION AND BULL IN FIGHTING STANCE. PAINTING DRAWN IN THE MANNER OF MUHAMMAD SIYAH-QALAM.
MIDDLE TO SECOND HALF OF 15TH CENTURY. FOLIO 90 VERSO, HAZINE 2160, TOPKAPU SARAYI LIBRARY, ISTANBUL.

technical proficiency, and spirit of these paintings, although the precise locality of their inspiration still remains unknown. They would thus represent the art of an accomplished painter in Herat, one of the great urban art centers, reflecting at the same time the artist's experiences in a more easterly tribal area.

There are a few paintings which, though roughly contemporary with these two major types of painting, do not belong to them stylistically or sociologically and probably come from different environments. There is, for instance, a powerful rendition of a fight between a lion and a bull which, unlike many other such representations—such as those in Achaemenian and Classical art—do not show the mighty lion on the back of the hapless victim who is seen felled by his fierce attack. Instead, the two animals face each other tensely like two prize fighters, the one ready to jump, the other, as if stupefied, considering how best to escape the dreaded attack. In the extraordinary foreshortening of the bodies, the delineation of the powerful muscles, and the psychological penetration of the mentality of the two antagonists this masterpiece uses means of expression unparalleled in the wider orbit of Islamic art. Here again we are in the dark about the exact region where such a painting could have been made. And the same applies to two other remarkable miniatures. The first of these represents a Negro slave who, with a long fly whisk, is apparently attending a tethered horse seen rolling on the ground. Here the artist was eager to show the curious foreshortening of an animal's body and its wild movements as well as the little-known physical appearance of a dark-skinned person.

The second picture is an uncommonly large and colorful painting which in rare fashion amalgamates features of three civilizations. There are elements—especially in the outdoor scene on the left—which are strongly reminiscent of China; the main theme takes place in a domed building, characteristic of Iran or Central Asia, with its typical colorful tilework and Arabic and Persian inscriptions in various scripts. And finally, there is a strong Christian element. The building is designated as a monastery in one of the Persian inscriptions which, with an obvious reference to the Eucharist, states that "in this monastery where we were given the beaker our desires were fulfilled by Christ and Mary," while another promises eventual salvation "for the end is well." Some of the wall paintings portrayed within this building also allow a Christian interpretation. One on the lower floor to the left represents the "Meeting of Joachim and Anna at the Gate" while the third scene depicts "Christ Riding into Jerusalem." In the second story the representation on the left could easily be interpreted as "Christ Preaching to the Apostles"; even in the painting next to it which is partly covered by the dome one figure can be interpreted as Christ. The painting as a whole shows many monks studying and depicts other diverse aspects of a monastic milieu. Vividly portrayed as this rendition is, it shows many features which are unusual for a Western conception of a monastery; only the emaciated figure of a half-clad hermit close to the door on the right reminds us of the traditional Western figures of John the Baptist and other desert saints. It is a skillful amalgamation of elements from various civilizations and presents them in most explicit manner since according to the Persian fashion the painting shows three sides of the building and life in the interior and the exterior as well. To judge from the type of the Christian wall paintings which are related to certain historical miniatures of Herat, one would assume that a picture such as this might well have been executed about 1425 or shortly thereafter and in a region strongly permeated by Iranian civilization but yet open to pervasive Chinese and Christian influences coming from somewhere in Central Asia—all of which points again to Herat or the area around it.

SCENE IN A CENTRAL ASIAN MONASTERY. POSSIBLY HERAT, SECOND QUARTER OF 15TH CENTURY. FOLIO 131 VERSO, HAZINE 2153, TOPKAPU SARAYI LIBRARY, ISTANBUL.

The same albums which contain the weird though highly accomplished pictures of a primitive inner-Asiatic society include many more samples of the sophisticated and complex art of Iran itself. They are particularly rich and illuminating with regard to the first phase of truly Persian miniature painting which represents the amalgamation of the earlier Seljuk pictorial style with that of China. This stage was reached under the reign of the Mongol ruler Abu Sa'id (1317-1335); according to tradition, its successful accomplishment was due to the efforts of a master called Ahmed Musa who is said to have "withdrawn the covering from the face of painting and invented the kind of painting" which then became generally current in Iran. One of the manuscripts attributed to him is a *Book of the Ascension (Mi'rāj-nameh)*. A number of miniatures which seem to have come from this work were at some later time cut from the pages with accompanying text and pasted in one of the albums. They show the legendary experiences of Muhammad and especially the various stages of his ascent to heaven during which he is borne upward on the shoulders of the Archangel Gabriel, encounters prophets, and finally arrives at the Heavenly Gate beyond which the vision of the Tree of Paradise awaits him and the visions that lie beyond it. These paintings are rendered in a dramatic and monumental style and executed with strong colors. One of the miniatures which shows the Prophet being carried heavenwards by the Archangel in the company of minor angels makes it dramatically clear that in their journey they have already passed high above snow-covered mountains which are still visible between golden sheaths of flames outlined with red and black. This miraculous ascension has never been portrayed more vividly in the Muslim sphere. It reflects a widely diffused Islamic literature on the otherworldly experiences of the Prophet which was even known to medieval Europe in Spanish, French, and Latin translations and forms a parallel to Dante's poetical visions of Paradise and Hell. Other paintings in these albums illustrate the more commonly rendered epic past of Iran; love scenes occur as well and the rarely treated fabulous accounts of travelers and other folkloristic tales. The albums of course abound in the ornate, more detailed and romantically conceived Persian paintings of the fifteenth and sixteenth centuries; although these, too, are a visual delight and greatly enrich our knowledge, they are not quite as spectacular as the rarer paintings from the earliest stage of Persian miniature painting in the first half of the fourteenth century.

Two more Iranian objects which must have come into Turkish possession during one of the sixteenth-century campaigns are remarkable in their different ways; both are also of a type of which nothing exists any longer in Iran itself. The first is a large circular shield with rich mother-of-pearl inlays representing royal throne scenes and hunting subjects for which the iridescent material was a most appropriate though difficult medium. This piece now in the Hall of Arms and Armor in the Topkapu Sarayı Museum is certainly an object of great luxury which may be one of the earliest in which this particular inlay material was used. Since it later became very popular in Turkey, one wonders whether the technique may not have been stimulated by

THE PROPHET MUHAMMAD CARRIED HEAVENWARDS BY THE ARCHANGEL GABRIEL IN THE COMPANY OF OTHER ANGELS. IRAN, ABOUT 1320-1325.
FOLIO 42 VERSO, HAZINE 2154, TOPKAPU SARAYI LIBRARY, ISTANBUL.

this very shield. But unlike the later Turkish objects which use the mother-of-pearl primarily in rather large square, oblong, or round units, the more intricate designs of this piece made much higher demands on the artistic and technical abilities of the master craftsman. The other object is an elegantly shaped, long-necked zinc bottle whose mat ground is inlaid with delicately wrought scenes of fighting animals in gold. The sumptuous aspect of the piece is further enriched by incrustations of rubies and turquoises placed within the large medallions of the body and on the slender neck both of which are densely covered with a network of cut-out arabesques. Animal subjects executed with the same finesse occur also in contemporary Persian book illuminations, textiles, and carpets but not in metalwork; when used there they are much coarser. Such zinc objects were also made in Turkey, though in view of Ottoman disinclination to use human or animal figures in the decorative arts they are usually ornamented with arabesques and floral designs only. The application of precious and semi-precious stones was also of course a favorite Turkish technique. There is definitely a close connection between the Safavid and Ottoman examples, but it is still impossible to say who first developed this type of metalwork.

BRASS BASIN INLAID WITH GOLD AND SILVER, MADE FOR THE MAMLUK SULTAN QA'ITBAY (1468-1496). EGYPT, END OF 15TH CENTURY. MUSEUM OF TURKISH AND ISLAMIC ART, ISTANBUL.

SHIELD WITH MOTHER-OF-PEARL INLAYS. IRAN, SECOND HALF OF 16TH CENTURY.
ARMOR HALL, TOPKAPU SARAYI MUSEUM, ISTANBUL.

ZINC BOTTLE WITH GOLD INLAYS AND INCRUSTATIONS OF RUBIES AND TURQUOISES. IRAN, 16TH CENTURY.
TREASURY OF THE TOPKAPU SARAYI MUSEUM, ISTANBUL.

The booty taken by Selim I from Cairo after his conquest of Egypt in 1517 was also remarkable. An early piece is an 'alam or finial, apparently originally used to top a minaret. This carries the name of the Mamluk Sultan al-Muayyad (1412-1422) whose mosque near the eleventh-century gate called Bab Zuweila is still one of the sights of the city. It is made of gilded brass and terminates in a *hilal* or crescent. Thus it is the earliest preserved object in this form from a religious setting and antedates many others of indeterminate period on the numerous Istanbul minarets as well as the representations of mosques in Italian paintings such as those of Carpaccio which use the same emblem as a crowning element. The presence of such an object in Istanbul and its preservation in the Hall of Arms and Armor of the Imperial Palace underlines the symbolic significance of its capture. Just as a cross on a church tower was replaced by a crescent when the building was turned into a mosque after the capture of a town or when part of a Christian building was incorporated into a Muslim one, so does this finial exemplify the Ottoman victory and assure its duration.

Another "foreign" artifact, now in the Istanbul Museum of Turkish and Islamic Art, represents what is generally admitted to be the finest extant piece of metalwork of the final period of medieval Egyptian art. It is a brass basin with well-preserved gold and silver inlays and is inscribed with the name of Qa'itbay (1468-1496), the last great independent ruler of the country. This sultan came into conflict with Mehmet the Conqueror and the latter's son Bayazid II, but he also exchanged embassies with them; it is assumed, however, that this basin probably formed part of Selim I's booty from Egypt, the character of which was vividly described by the contemporary Egyptian historian Ibn Iyas: "Selim left Egypt with a thousand camels, laden partly with gold, partly with silver—apart from what he looted of rare things, weapons, porcelains, and hammered copper ... even the famous marble was moved away. He took away from there always the best of everything, things which neither his fathers nor his ancestors before him had ever enjoyed." The basin is decorated with a technical ability unusual for the time. Its interior shows the typical Mamluk design of a complex geometric star composition developed from a central element and made to branch out into a wreath of other such partially shown units. The exterior presents the royal name and titles within an elaborate border of arabesques, which are of a type subsequently introduced into Venetian metalwork by Muslim artisans. Whatever its early history may have been, the geometric composition of the interior should have greatly appealed to its new Turkish owners for precisely the same design had been used in Anatolia since Seljuk times and continued to be favored in the sixteenth and seventeenth centuries for *mimbers* and pieces of furniture, although usually without the varied filling devices in the star designs.

In conclusion one other category of exotic objects in Istanbul should be mentioned: the Chinese porcelains which are known to all visitors to the Topkapu Palace as they present an overwhelming display in the old imperial kitchens built by Sinan. The

Chinese had always had a great reputation for the excellence of their art, as is expressed for instance by the geographer Ibn al-Faqih (about 903 A.D.): "God has distinguished the people of China by special perfection in handicrafts and he has given to them what he has given to nobody else. Thus they have Chinese silk, Chinese porcelain vessels, and Chinese lamps, and other perfect things of a similar kind, admirable in execution, exact in production." Muslim intellectuals were also fully aware of the infinite care with which pottery was made in China in contrast to the Near Eastern imitations. Aesthetic appreciation was, however, not the only reason for the great interest in Chinese porcelains, since the Persian scientist and writer Nasir eddin at-Tusi informs us (in the second half of the thirteenth century) that "if one put poison into such vessels, sweat is found on it." Nor is this all, for the Turkish merchant Ali Ekber, who was in China from 1505 to 1508, states in the book dealing with his experiences there that "to eat and drink from Chinese porcelains improves the vitality." It is clear how valuable such beautiful and efficacious tableware must have been to Near Eastern grandees and potentates forever fearful of the loss of their "vitality" or worse, their very lives. From this it follows also that such expensive wares when amassed in large numbers—especially those of large size and beautiful execution—became what today would be termed status symbols. Chinese porcelains were accordingly used in many different places, as the descriptions of Muslim writers attest, and sherds from such pieces have been discovered at a number of Islamic sites which date from hundreds of years before porcelain became known in Europe.

The first datable early porcelains were excavated in Samarra, on the Tigris, the ninth-century capital of the Abbasid caliphs, although we have even earlier reports on the import of Chinese wares to the Near East; great stores including large vessels for washing clothes were owned by the Fatimid caliphs of Cairo in the eleventh century. The great Saladin presented Chinese porcelain pieces to his overlord in Syria, and Qa'itbay (whose inlaid basin we have just discussed) sent the same type of present to Lorenzo de' Medici in Florence. To speak of still existing collections one should refer to Shah Abbas of Iran who in 1611 gave 1,162 pieces to his ancestral shrine in Ardabil. But the greatest assemblage of them all, about 8,000 pieces, is the one in Istanbul. It is by far the largest collection of Chinese pottery from the Sung to the Ching period outside the Far East and contains besides celadons and white wares a celebrated collection of blue-and-white vessels from the Yüan period on. The celadons alone number 1,300, of which the earliest belong to the Sung period, and there are 2,600 examples of blue-and-white ware mainly of the Yüan and Ming periods. Nothing of this collection existed in Byzantine times and it is therefore an Ottoman creation. The earliest pieces, five in number, are listed in an inventory of 1495 made during the reign of Bayazid II, and thirty-two more pieces arrived in the Palace Treasury in the early sixteenth century. The real impetus came with an additional sixty-two pieces which were taken by Selim I from the Hesht Bihisht Palace in Tabriz conquered in 1514 and again when the camel loads of Egyptian booty arrived in Constantinople

VASE OF DOUBLE-GOURD SHAPE PAINTED WITH BLUE PEONY SCROLLS ON A WHITE GROUND.
CHINA, 14TH CENTURY, WITH TURKISH SILVER COVER OF THE 18TH CENTURY. TOPKAPU SARAYI MUSEUM, ISTANBUL.

after 1517. Seventy plates bear the mark of the Emperor Chia-ching (1522-1566), the contemporary of Süleyman the Magnificent, and the dates to be attributed to later wares as well as occasional references to additions in the seventeenth century demonstrate the constant growth of the collection. A huge inventory of some 10,000 pieces was made in 1762 to 1792, and this is generally regarded as the terminal date.

By common consent the earliest blue-and-white wares of the fourteenth century, comprising huge dishes with diameters up to 18½ inches, large bowls, and tall vases of various shapes, are the most intriguing and their designs of flowers, animals, and formal patterns are probably the most handsome. The tallest of the vases, of the double gourd variety (with a height of 28 inches) may well be called characteristic of the group. Its beautiful display of freely moving scrolls of peony flowers and the curiously shaped long leaves which the Yüan potters combined with these blooms is typical for the style of this group; the only unusual element is the eighteenth-century Turkish silver edging at the top onto which a domed cover is screwed. This is only one of many such pieces which vary from case to case and in all instances reveal different designs splendidly executed in deep "Muhammedan Blue." Any person sensitive to design and skillful ceramic composition must be impressed by the massed effect of this superb collection from a foreign land.

Our survey thus terminates in the ancient capital city on the Bosphorus and the many wonders to be seen there today. There is no way of telling what other surprises Istanbul, this great treasure-house of all the arts, still has in store for us. Whatever they may be they will reflect the far-flung history of this second Rome and its unique and enchanting geographical position: "on European soil, but looking toward Asia, with Egypt and Africa away to the right—connected with all the world by land and by sea."

INDEX OF NAMES AND PLACES

LIST OF ILLUSTRATIONS

INDEX OF NAMES AND PLACES

LIST OF ILLUSTRATIONS

THE EARLIEST CIVILIZATIONS OF ANATOLIA

BYZANTIUM

THIS BOOK WAS DESIGNED AND PRODUCED BY THE TECHNICAL
STAFF OF EDITIONS D'ART ALBERT SKIRA. FINISHED THE TENTH
DAY OF SEPTEMBER NINETEEN HUNDRED AND SIXTY-SIX.

TEXT AND ILLUSTRATIONS PRINTED BY THE

COLOR STUDIOS
IMPRIMERIES RÉUNIES, LAUSANNE.

COLOR PLATES ENGRAVED BY GUEZELLE & RENOUARD, PARIS.
BLACK AND WHITE PLATES BY ROTO-SADAG S.A., GENEVA.

All the photographs in this book are by
MAURICE BABEY, BASEL

*except those on pages 37, 93, 176, 183 (Ara Güler, Istanbul), page 58 (Archaeo-
logical Museum, Istanbul), page 65 (Theresa Goell, New York), page 80
(Trinity College Library, Cambridge), page 112 (Bibliothèque Nationale,
Paris), page 160 (Walter Steinkopf, Berlin), and page 190 (Smithsonian
Institution, National Collection of Fine Arts, Washington, D.C.).*

PRINTED IN SWITZERLAND